GW00506069

total body *transformation*

Michelle Bridges has worked in the health and fitness industry for over 20 years as a professional trainer and group fitness instructor. Her key role in Channel Ten's hit TV show *The Biggest Loser* combined with her highly successful online exercise and mindset program, the 12 Week Body Transformation, has connected her with hundreds of thousands of Australians, making her this country's most recognised and influential health and fitness personality. *Crunch Time* was her first book. She has since produced eight others — *Crunch Time Cookbook, Losing the Last 5 Kilos, 5 Minutes a Day, The No Excuses Cookbook, Everyday Weight Loss, Your Best Body, Get Real!* and *Superfoods Cookbook*. All have been bestsellers.

michellebridges.com.au

michelle bridges

total body
transformation

lose weight fast and keep it off

VIKING
an imprint of
PENGUIN BOOKS

To every one of the thousands of people from all over the world who have trusted me to help change their lives — I have learnt so much from you. You are my inspiration!

VIKING

Published by the Penguin Group
Penguin Group (Australia)
707 Collins Street, Melbourne, Victoria 3008, Australia
(a division of Penguin Australia Pty Ltd)
Penguin Group (USA) Inc.
375 Hudson Street, New York, New York 10014, USA
Penguin Group (Canada)
90 Eglinton Avenue East, Suite 700, Toronto, Canada ON M4P 2Y3
(a division of Penguin Canada Books Inc.)
Penguin Books Ltd
80 Strand, London WC2R 0RL England
Penguin Ireland
25 St Stephen's Green, Dublin 2, Ireland
(a division of Penguin Books Ltd)
Penguin Books India Pvt Ltd
11 Community Centre, Panchsheel Park, New Delhi 110 017, India
Penguin Group (NZ)
67 Apollo Drive, Rosedale, Auckland 0632, New Zealand
(a division of Penguin New Zealand Pty Ltd)
Penguin Books (South Africa) (Pty) Ltd
Rosebank Office Park, Block D, 181 Jan Smuts Avenue, Parktown North, Johannesburg 2196, South Africa
Penguin (Beijing) Ltd
7F, Tower B, Jiaming Center, 27 East Third Ring Road North, Chaoyang District, Beijing 100020, China

Penguin Books Ltd, Registered Offices: 80 Strand, London WC2R 0RL, England

First published by Penguin Group (Australia), 2014

10 9 8 7 6 5 4 3 2 1

Text and photography copyright © Michelle Bridges, 2014
Food photography copyright © Penguin Group (Australia), 2014

The moral right of the author has been asserted

All rights reserved. Without limiting the rights under copyright reserved above, no part of this publication may be reproduced, stored in or introduced into a retrieval system, or transmitted, in any form or by any means (electronic, mechanical, photocopying, recording or otherwise), without the prior written permission of both the copyright owner and the above publisher of this book.

Cover and text design by Adam Laszczuk © Penguin Group (Australia)
Photography by Henryk Lobaczewski
Food photography by Julie Renouf, home economy by Caroline Jones, food styling by Georgia Young, photographer's assistant Linda Oliveri
Typeset in Mundo Sans by Pauline Hass © Penguin Group (Australia)
Colour separation by Splitting Image, Clayton, Victoria
Printed and bound in China by 1010 Printing Group Ltd.

National Library of Australia Cataloguing-in-Publication data:
Bridges, Michelle.
Michelle Bridges' total body transformation / Michelle Bridges.
ISBN: 9780670078134 (paperback)
1. Exercise. 2. Health. 3. Weight loss.

613.7

penguin.com.au

While every care has been taken in researching and compiling the dietary and exercise information in this book, it is in no way intended to replace or supersede professional medical advice. Neither the author nor the publisher may be held responsible for any action or claim howsoever resulting from the use of this book or any information contained in it. Readers must obtain their own professional medical advice before relying on or otherwise making used of the dietary and exercise information in this book.

contents

taking control   1

get *real!*

1   no more excuses!   6

2   what you resist persists   13

3   breaking old habits   21

4   you gotta have a plan, man!   32

get *moving!*

5   body basics   44

6   calories in, calories out   48

7   debunking the myths   55

8   enough talk, action!   60

9   exercises that work   74

10   workout program   114

get *cooking!*

11   nutrition   136

12   your kitchen makeover   151

13   a sample eating plan   154

14   recipes   158

15   eating out   224

staying on track   228

'new you' journal   229

acknowledgements   231

selected references   231

index   232

total body transformation total body transformation total body transformation total body transformation total body transformation

taking control

'together we'll get you where you want to go'

WOW, WHAT A JOURNEY IT'S BEEN SO FAR. When *Crunch Time* was first published I was bowled over by the response. It seemed that there were many people who were looking to take control of their lives and get healthy. I feel so privileged and proud that I could play a part in helping people achieve their goals.

Crunch Time became the inspiration for reaching people online, and the core messages of getting your head right, eating well and exercising regularly contained in these pages became the central themes for the 12 Week Body Transformation program, or 12WBT. At the time of writing, these messages have supported 12WBT participants in losing over 500 000 kilos and living happier, healthier lives.

As I've published other books and connected with a whole community online, I have been so inspired by the stories of men and women turning their lives around, embracing the pleasures, joys (and challenges!) of a healthy diet and regular exercise. The more I've travelled, meeting people who have made positive changes in their lives, the more convinced I have become that taking control of your body is the way to a happier life.

Over recent years, Australia has grown, literally, to become one of the most overweight countries on earth. We may have a reputation for sporting prowess, but it seems that too few of us are exercising enough. Combined with an explosion in fast food consumption, that makes for a pretty weighty nation. The good news is that it's within our power to do something about it. There has never been a better time to get real, get moving and change our bodies — and in doing so, change our lives.

When it comes to weight loss and fitness, nothing is set in stone. From the very first moment you make a healthy choice over an unhealthy one, you are improving yourself. Making active decisions about the food you eat and the amount of exercise you do will transform your body, your energy levels, your outlook and your future.

Many individuals have found that the results and rewards of choosing to be healthy are amazing. And you can do it too. You've bought this book because you feel the need for change. I'm going to help you make it. **Whether you want to lose 5 kilos or 50 kilos, this book will show you how.** It's going to be hard work, but if you commit to the workouts and follow the nutrition plan you *will* see drastic changes in your body. But only *you* can make the change — the book can't do it. I can't do it. No one can do it except you.

This kind of dramatic change will take you well out of your comfort zone, but let me ask you something: which discomfort would you prefer? The 'I hate the way I look, I can't fit into anything and I feel like crap' kind, or the 'I'd better get my runners on and take the dog for a run and tonight I'll have grilled fish with no alcohol for dinner' kind? Which of these scenarios is *really* the most uncomfortable?

Once you have the nutrition and the exercise in place, weight loss is an exercise in mathematics; for most of us it's pretty much calories in versus calories out. But *The Biggest Loser* taught me that you *cannot* expect to lose weight and keep it off if you're still carrying emotional baggage. **If you do not deal with the psychological aspect of weight loss, the physical just isn't going to happen.**

In the first section, 'Get Real', I will help you get your head sorted so you can address the emotional issues behind your struggle with your weight. Let me tell you — most people don't get messed up in the head because they are overweight; they become overweight because they are messed up in the head. If you are going to find the solution to managing your weight permanently, then all the diet and exercise books in the world won't help unless you re-program the way you think about food, exercise and ultimately yourself.

In the second section, 'Get Moving', I will guide you through a series of killer workouts. I have worked in the fitness industry all my life

'*show me someone who put the weight back on because they lost it too quickly and I'll show you five people who put the weight back on because they lost it too slowly!*'

and I know the best exercises for *rapid* weight loss. But I'm not going to lie to you — in most cases it took *years* for you to put the weight on, so it's going to take real guts and determination to lose it. You absolutely must follow the exercise and nutrition plan for at least twelve weeks. Some of you will reach your goal weight before twelve weeks, others may need to continue for a few extra weeks, but whatever your individual needs, **this program works!**

In 'Get Cooking', I show you how to minimise calories and maximise your nutrition. There is no way on this planet that you can accelerate yourself to lean and mean unless you put in some time in the kitchen, so I've included some of my favourite recipes.

I'm here to help you find the real 'you' — the person who knows what they want and knows how to get it. You'll be your own personal trainer with this book, but you won't be alone. Let me lay it on the line for you — your struggles are my struggles. Your demons are my demons. I have battled with my weight just as you have. But I will not tell you what you want to hear. I will give it to you straight, because I am standing right there beside you in this. *I understand.* But what I want from you in exchange for this empathy is your trust and commitment.

No more excuses.

No more laying the blame at someone else's feet.

No more lying to yourself. It's time to be true to you. And I will be here, every step of the way to guide you through it.

LET'S ROCK!

get real!

1
no
more
excuses!

*'taking weight off is science,
but keeping it off is psychology'*

IT'S TIME TO GIVE UP THE EXCUSES, PEOPLE!
You know – the ones you've been dragging
out for so long that you actually believe them,
and that you've even managed to get everyone
around you to believe too!

If you hear your wife/husband/friends/
kids saying 'she's always struggled with her
weight, her parents were both big people', or
'he'd love to exercise but he's got bad knees',
then you can safely assume that you've done
the perfect sell job. By enrolling others in your
denial, you've avoided facing up to uncomfortable issues, or even quietly blamed these
people as being part of the problem. You've
built a world for yourself where no one is
acknowledging what's real.

Takeaway is *not* cheaper!

I worked with one young woman who had what I call a 'light bulb' moment when she realised that she had actually talked herself into believing it was cheaper to buy takeaway pizza than cook at home. She really believed it until we worked through it and of course nailed the most critical element – dollars and cents. The pizza was $18, and usually came with specials on crappy soft drinks and garlic bread. By contrast, I showed her how she could put together a healthy meal at home for just $8, with enough left over for lunch the following day (a much tastier choice than leftover pizza!) The money she saved by cooking at home and not buying junk food could pay for a gym membership, a new pair of runners or even a personal trainer!

Here are some excuses I hear quite a bit – do any of them sound familiar?

- 'I can't exercise because I have a sore knee.'
- 'I'm too busy to eat breakfast.'
- 'I can't cook healthy food because my husband/kids won't eat it.'
- 'Being big-boned runs in my family.'
- 'I'm too tired to go to the gym at night.'

Maybe some of the excuses are based around finance: you know, 'I can't afford a gym membership or a personal trainer', or 'Healthy food is too expensive'. Financial imperatives can be tricky because they can be hard to ignore. When you're looking at financial excuses, make sure you compare the cost in real dollars.

However, the excuse that I hear the most is 'I'm too busy'. It gets dragged out by everyone, and therein lies a pertinent fact. We're all busy. People who are regular exercisers are busy. People who never exercise are busy. Very few of us would feel we have enough free time to stroll casually down to the gym for a workout or even to take a jog. But interestingly, often the busiest people in our society are the ones who exercise the most.

I mean, even prime ministers and presidents take regular exercise. So ask yourself, are you busier than a prime minister? I doubt it. Are there other things that leaders of entire nations could be doing for that precious hour? Of course there are – only about a million of them. Yet they still make exercise a priority in their lives as they recognise its importance to

'talking is good, but it should set the stage for action, not become a replacement for it'

health, work and family. Now apply that thinking to your own life.

I work with many women who believe that making time for exercise amounts to putting themselves before their family, yet are resentful and angry that they are at 'the bottom of the list'. I ask them, 'If your priority is your family, doesn't it make more sense to offer them a "better" version of yourself? Wouldn't they prefer a mum who is happy, confident and energised, rather than a tidy house?'

We're all busy. Your task is to make exercise part of your everyday life, just like brushing your teeth and making your bed. How badly do you want to do it? My Grampsy used to say, 'You can always find another hour in the day if you set the alarm clock an hour earlier!' It might mean you need to go to bed instead of watching TV, which by the way isn't going to get you *any* closer to your goal.

playing the victim
Cast your mind back to when you were a small child. Did you ever burst into tears to make people feel sorry for you so that you could get your own way? If it worked, and you repeated it enough, it became a behaviour pattern that you could potentially use for the rest of your life.

When you hear yourself coming out with comments like 'It's okay for her, she's naturally

slim' or, 'If only I didn't have the kids I could exercise' then the 'victim' alarm bells should be ringing, especially if you take your victimhood to the next level by seeming really upset. Your distress will ensure that others do not challenge your excuses, and you get to stay in your old patterns.

As a victim, you'll also have 'villains' — the people or things you believe are 'responsible' for your poor diet and exercise. It's only when you stop blaming people or circumstances for your unhappiness that you can empower yourself to create the new you. There is no room for victims on my team.

you decide *your* future
Now I want you to think about a time in your past when you realised how unhappy you were with your weight, health and fitness. It might be last week or it could go right back to your childhood. Take a moment to really reflect on this time in your life, and recall how you felt. Was it connected with a particular event, or with disparaging remarks from others? Recall other, similar defining moments, even ones you had hoped to forget. Roll them around in your mind. How did you feel? What decision did you make about yourself? What self-limiting beliefs did you form? Stop, close your eyes and take a few minutes with this.

'unless you're prepared to make a change in the present, your future can only reflect your past'

total body transformation total body transformation total body transformation total body transformation total body transformation total body transformation

Kirstie's game

I once met a young woman who had been struggling with her weight for most of her life. Kirstie had just got married and had lost a substantial amount of weight for the wedding, only to put it all back on again in the months afterwards. Her question to me was, 'How do you control those thoughts you get when you just become fixated on having to eat a certain food? Once I think of something I cannot stop thinking about it, and no matter what I do, I always buckle in the end.' She went on to explain that she was just over it — weary from the constant battle.

I addressed her last comments first. 'It sounds to me like you are at a crossroads. It's time for you to choose between getting the weight off for good, or being happy the way you are. The never-ending cycle of losing weight, putting it back on and beating yourself up is destroying you.' However, I knew there was definitely more to this story.

She explained that she had the 'all or nothing' approach and went nuts for the wedding, but just let it slide again afterwards. 'I don't know how to stop that craving! Once it's in my head, I can't let it go. It's like I have no control, it is totally out of my hands!'

I hear this *so* often. I knew what to say.

'This is your game. You play it so you can claim that you have no responsibility. The game allows you to be a victim and blame something else, like your body's craving, rather than face the fact that *you are the one in charge*. Acknowledge it now and fight back, one craving at a time. Each time you beat it, you take back a little more control. Each time you win you get a little more power. Self-control = self-respect. While you continue to play the victim you have no power at all. No self-control = no self-respect.'

She told me that she was still working with her personal trainer, but that her weight continued to creep up. I asked her if she had ever kept a seven-day food diary. She said, 'Yes, I have, but I lied on it. I didn't want to see my trainer go through it with a red pen.' Bam! There it was. She had been lying to herself all along. What you resist persists. What you deny gets bigger. It was the first time in a while that she had got this real with herself, and for her the relief fuelled her empowerment.

It was only a brief talk, and it by no means solved everything in one hit, but her acknowledgement was the first step towards change.

Change your thinking, change your world.

Now, here's the clincher. The beliefs you formed about yourself in the past dictate your behaviour today. And unless you're prepared to make a change in the present, your future can only reflect your past.

Your future needs to be decided now, and to do that you must ask yourself some questions about what you want. What kind of future would excite, move and inspire you? If you wish to have that future, what are you prepared to change *right now*?

what is really holding you back?

If you've been to this place in the past, but freeze up when you get to the part about making a change, you need to ask yourself 'What is holding me back?' Maybe you get 'paralysis by analysis' and overanalyse to the extent that it all becomes too complex and you become overwhelmed. Or maybe you simply don't know if you have the strength to do it. And before you know it, all the negative self-talk and the tired excuses flood back in and you shelve the whole idea: 'I'll get to that next week/month/year.' We all want it right now, but achieving it starts with action, not words.

why get up for that morning jog?

- Because your mind and your body will function better for it.
- Because you'll probably live quite a bit longer.
- Because you'll be less likely to live your later years with chronic disability, draining the emotions and finances of those around you.
- Because you won't be that resentful mum/dad/wife/husband/partner who feels like they never get time for themselves (ouch!)
- But most important of all, you will be healthier *and* happier. (Many, *many* studies prove the effectiveness of exercise in managing depression.)

'most people don't get messed up in the head because they're overweight — they become overweight because they're messed up in the head'

Some people say they want to lose weight desperately, but they never convert their intentions into actions. Is this you? If it is, I want you to ask yourself what is it that you are afraid of; what is it about the 'action' that scares you?

- Are you afraid of change? Of not being able to eat all the food you eat now? Well, my answer to that is simple: what the hell is so scary about that? You're clearly not starving! And I promise you — your new eating habits will help you lose weight *and* save you time and money.
- Does the thought of exercise send you into a blind panic? We're talking profound life-extending change here, so it's definitely not time to be sooky! *Please!* Exercise is nothing to be afraid of. Earthquakes, accidents and war — yes; exercise — no.
- Or are you scared to fail? That's an easy one — the greatest opportunities for learning happen through screw-ups, especially if you are ready and willing to learn from them.

Sometimes when I'm talking to people struggling with their weight, it's as if they think that as long as they keep *talking* about weight loss it will somehow magically happen. Talking is good, but it should be setting the stage for action, not become a replacement for it. It has to lead to something. **Remember: thoughts, words, *action!***

If any of these fears ring true for you, then you need to face up squarely to them — bring them out into the open. Because when you acknowledge something, that's the first step to owning it, and in doing so, taking responsibility for it. You will no longer be able to put the blame on others or use all those well-honed excuses. *You* are in charge of the new you.

2
what you resist persists

'the truth will set you free'

THE MORE WE RESIST SOMETHING, the more it comes back to haunt us. This is because by trying to push it away we're actually giving it a lot of attention — and it stays foremost in our minds. It's only when we stand in front of it, face it and stare it down that we can take the first step towards getting it out of our lives.

So, what have you been resisting? Are you:

- living in denial about your size?
- feeling deeply unhappy about your body?
- unable to admit that you overeat?
- aware that you should be exercising, but refuse to incorporate it into your life?

Resistance equals persistence. The more you push these things away, the bigger and louder they get, so that overcoming them seems even *more* daunting.

In order to break the cycle you need to do the opposite of hiding from them — you must embrace them.

- *Embrace* that you are overweight.
- *Embrace* that you eat too much.
- *Embrace* that you don't like to exercise.
- *Embrace* that you make excuses about yourself.

And when I say 'embrace' I mean 'accept' — hold these truths close, hug them and understand them without blaming yourself — just accept responsibility for them. *Own* that you choose to be who you are today.

It's only when you take total ownership of the way you are that you can move forward. These truths are about *you*. Just be with them; stop beating yourself up.

digging deep

To embrace these truths, you have to *find* them, and believe me, sometimes they're buried deep. To dig them out you need to answer some difficult questions. But timing is of the essence. It's got to be the right time for you to do this. **You must be open to the process and have enough self-respect to be completely honest with yourself.** Because let me tell you, the real damage occurs when you keep saying you are ready, but in fact you are not.

People who haven't thoroughly done the mental and emotional stuff – who haven't properly dealt with the bigger issues, the inner demons, the negative self-talk, the excuses – usually fall off the wagon and then beat themselves up about it. Does this sound like you? That cycle is far more damaging than overeating and not exercising will ever be, because every time you do this, you chip away at your self-confidence, your self-worth, your inner warrior. I see so many women and men racked with guilt, frustrated and full of self-hate because they are on a never-ending cycle of on-again, off-again diet and exercise. So I ask you again: are you ready to come clean?

For most of my life I have been an active person, but after having children I had become lethargic, overweight and quite frankly, lazy. I loved my family, but not who I had become. Changing my life and putting my trust in Michelle's advice was one of the hardest decisions I've ever made because for the first time I had to put myself before my children and partner.

It was a risk worth taking. Michelle changed my entire outlook on life. For the first time ever I focused on myself completely. Michelle taught me about self-discipline and self-worth. She taught me how to incorporate good nutrition and proper exercise into my busy life, and it was so much easier than I thought. Michelle has been my saviour. The support, motivation and knowledge that she has given me are things that I will never take for granted.

Thanks, Mish, for helping me become a happier person, but more importantly a better (and more beautiful) mother and wife.

Deb, 35

*'you can only really fail by not doing anything;
being honest with yourself is the first crucial step
to making positive changes to your life'*

Okay. Here goes. Take a notebook, and complete each statement as shown below. Take it slowly, preferably completing one before you move on to the next. When you decide your action, rate your commitment level on a scale of 1 to 10. Maybe sit with a close friend, personal trainer, life coach or even a therapist (if you have one) if you are worried about being really honest. But it has got to be someone who knows your background, and has enough clarity to help you uncover the truth about yourself.

1. *I am overweight because I . . .*
   the actions I'm taking to change this right now are . . . *my commitment level is . . .*

2. *I overeat because I . . .*
   the actions I'm taking to change this right now are . . . *my commitment level is . . .*

3. *I turn to food when things go bad/good because I . . .*
   the actions I'm taking to change this right now are . . . *my commitment level is . . .*

4. *I pretend I don't care, when I really do because I . . .*
   the actions I'm taking to change this right now are . . . *my commitment level is . . .*

5. *I eat alone or behind closed doors because I . . .*
   the actions I'm taking to change this right now are . . . *my commitment level is . . .*

6. *I beat myself up after I've overeaten because I . . .*
   the actions I'm taking to change this right now are . . . *my commitment level is . . .*

7. *I always put weight back on again after losing it because I . . .*
   the actions I'm taking to change this right now are . . . *my commitment level is . . .*

8. *I don't take better care of myself because I . . .*
   the actions I'm taking to change this right now are . . . *my commitment level is . . .*

How did you go? Did you do them all? Don't leave blank spaces thinking I'll come back to that later, because you won't. No cutting corners! That's how you got into this mess in the first place. And don't try giving me any 'I don't know' answers. That will not cut it. This is *your life* we are talking about. Finish the task properly. **Self-awareness is the first step to change.**

How you completed the first part of each statement helps you identify the stories you've told yourself about why you are where you are right now. The second part (your action and commitment level) will give you an action plan to help you get started and also give you a damn good indication of how badly you want it.

If this introspection has resulted in some enlightenment, a couple of 'oh my gods' or even a mini breakdown, then you're well on

the way to major change. Or perhaps you came to the conclusion that you're not ready to make the change, that your time isn't now — and that's okay too. **This is about you being okay with what you choose. It's about truly coming to terms with what you want, or don't want, and then absolutely choosing it — owning it.**

For example, you might be thinking:

I am not ready to undergo such a big lifestyle change. It's not a big enough priority. I'm not ready to give up my favourite foods and I don't want to exercise because I don't like it. I enjoy eating a lot of food and I don't want to stop. I am fully aware that my lifestyle choices have led me to become the size that I am and I accept the health implications that come with that. These are things I choose and I am honestly okay with them.

Or you might be thinking like this:

I am ready to ask some hard questions of myself and answer them with total honesty. I'm ready to take 100 per cent responsibility for my thoughts and actions. I know that my weight is holding me back and I want a different future for myself, so I'm going to make changes to my diet and learn more about nutrition. I want to feel better about myself and to be fitter, so I'm going to start an effective exercise program. Today I choose to do something different, and I'll choose it again tomorrow and the next day and for the rest of my life.

Munnalita's breakthrough

One of the best examples of a breakdown and subsequent breakthrough occurred during *The Biggest Loser* with a contestant called Munnalita. After a twist in the game, Munnalita had been given the very unpleasant task of sending one of the female contestants home. As difficult as this was, I support the principle behind making the contestants participate in challenges, as it mirrors the kind of tests they will face in real life. When things go wrong in the house, as they do in life, it can be the universe saying 'Okay, so you think you've got this weight issue under control, huh? Well try this on!'

It wasn't long before Munnalita found herself at the fridge. She was upset and she did just what she always did when she was upset – eat. It was a reflex action that had become an ingrained behaviour. At training the next morning she confided in me, and as she was telling me what had happened, her distress quickly turned to anger – she was angry at everything, especially herself, and it was obvious that she was well and truly sick of being overweight. Soon the entire history of her struggle with her weight started to pour out. It was raw and it was real, and I was sitting right in the middle of a breakdown. I knew that what had to be coming next was the breakthrough and I was right there to support her, but she had to find it on her own.

'Okay, Munnalita. What could you have done instead of going to the fridge?' I asked.

'What do you mean?' she sobbed.

Again, I quietly asked her what else she could have done.

'I don't know. I don't know what you mean!' she repeated.

I stayed with her, coaxing her softly.

'I don't know . . . I guess I could have sat on the lounge with everyone else . . .'

'Come on, Munnalita,' I said. 'What else could you have done besides go to the fridge?'

It took a while, but then suddenly through the tears and confusion her face lit up and she looked me in the eye and said almost in disbelief, 'I could have gone for a walk? Oh my God! I could have gone for a walk! I can't believe it! Imagine if every time I was upset I went for a walk instead of walking to the fridge! I'd be as skinny as you!'

She was so excited and although to me it was an obvious choice, to her it was an epiphany.

It was the best breakthrough I have ever witnessed, and such a powerful moment that I didn't want to let it go without giving her the opportunity to take the next step – action. So I asked her to consider the possibility that every time she felt upset she could go for a walk rather than open the fridge. While she pondered the idea I extended my hand and asked her to shake on it. The look of horror on her face was priceless. She quickly hid her hand behind her back.

'You can't be serious? You don't understand . . . if I shake on it that would mean . . . Oh, Michelle! You don't know what you are asking me!'

I stood my ground and kept my hand extended and my eyes fixed on hers.

'I can't do that! I mean, it's . . . it's what I've always done! If I shake on it then it's my word and I don't think I can do it!'

I knew she was feeling cornered, but I also knew that this was a pivotal moment. This was it.

'Munnalita, this is why we are here right now. This is why you are here in the house. Everything that has transpired in your life has led you to this point. What are you going to choose? What is it that you want? What sort of a future moves you? Are there children in that future?'

We stood there, Munnalita in tears with one hand behind her back, and me with my hand extended, for what seemed like ages. Then, finally, she took my hand and shook it. It was big stuff for her, as she was effectively saying goodbye to an old friend, something that she felt absolutely comfortable with and had been comforted by for many years.

I was overwhelmed with admiration for her; she was truly amazing! We stood holding each other in the garden while she let it all out, and when she was done she looked at me and thanked me through tear-filled eyes. What she didn't realise was that I had got as much out of the experience as she had, maybe even more, and I will always be grateful to her for that.

'what's the point of ruining your makeup if you don't learn something from the experience?'

You are now at a crossroad. You either choose it or you don't. Do yourself and everyone around you a favour — *don't say you will if you know you won't!* Be honest, either way. The key is to be truly okay with whichever choice you make.

with every breakdown there's a breakthrough

So how did it feel to be truthful about what's holding you back? Sometimes it takes a meltdown before you can get real and move forward to make the changes you want to make. An emotional breakdown opens you up. It pulls down all the guards and clears the pathway to exciting possibilities. It is often when you are at your rawest that you find clarity.

payoffs and costs

Being human means that we often do things because there is a payoff, a sweetener that makes it worth our while. Although you've now answered some very tough questions about why you are overweight, and about what you are prepared to do to change, there is one more very important question to answer. Have you ever considered that there might be a payoff for you being overweight? I know that sounds completely out there, but remember, we're asking the hard questions here, so check in

with yourself: what's in it for you? What's your kickback? Do you get to:

- Eat whatever you want, whenever you want, and take no responsibility for it?
- Get out of doing something by using your weight as an excuse?
- Use your weight to manipulate others?

It takes real courage to answer these questions, and it means you may have to face up to aspects of yourself that you're not proud of. But work through it — **it's all part of the journey.**

Okay, now — what is the cost of your being overweight/unfit/unhealthy? What are you missing out on, or losing?

Do you:

- Hate looking at yourself in the mirror?
- Never have anything to wear?
- Feel that you look ridiculous?
- Avoid going out?
- Push your partner away sexually because you're embarrassed about what you look like naked?
- Have health problems?

Grab your notebook and draw two columns. In the left-hand column list your payoffs. In the right-hand column list your costs. Take your time and be really honest. Now ask yourself: Are the payoffs really worth these costs?

3
breaking old habits

'self-control equals self-respect'

IF YOU WANT YOUR FUTURE to look different to your past (and by picking up this book, you obviously do), then you're going to need to start taking some different 'actions'. That isn't always easy — particularly if you have been doing the same 'actions' all your life.

Over the years I have worked with so many people who tell me they have arrived at a place of acceptance — embracing their weight and exercise issues — but that they are still unhappy, still overeating, still hating exercise and (naturally) still not losing weight. The reason for this is they have only reached the first step — facing their weight problem. They haven't understood that the next step is *action*. Without action, acceptance goes nowhere.

My yoghurt weakness

On my way to work I used to order a tub of yoghurt from my Greek mates, Anthony and Michael (aka the Greek Gods), who ran the local eatery near the gym. Man, that yoghurt was good. It was full of fat, of course, but I loved it and it soon became a habit three times a week. Then I noticed my butt taking on the same shape as the yoghurt tub, and I knew I needed to outmanoeuvre my weakness! I packed a piece of fruit in my gym bag and parked around the other side of the building so I didn't walk past the café. As I left the car and started walking in, I pulled out my piece of fruit and began eating it to take my mind off the yoghurt. I was effectively developing a different habit. It didn't take long for my new habit to kick in. It did, however, take some serious work to shift that yoghurt off my butt!

But here's some fantastic news! Most of your old actions were based around habits — the things that you do almost instinctively, which are just part of a routine or pattern of behaviour.

'What's so great about that?' I hear you ask. Well, it means you can form *new* habits! If you've done it before, you can do it again, except this time you're going to create supportive, powerful, healthy habits.

We make and break habits all the time. If you have been able to develop poor eating habits, then you are equally able to develop healthy ones. If you have developed a habit of not exercising, then you can easily learn to do the opposite.

What habits are holding you back? In your notebook list your 'Top 5 destructive habits'. Then replace each one with its opposite — an action that supports you — and practise, practise, PRACTISE!

There is a difference between having to do something and choosing to do it — you feel burdened when you have to do it, but you feel free when you *choose* to. Every day I make meal and exercise choices that keep me on track. I don't just let them happen around me or feel that I'm forced to do them. I *choose* them. It has taken me some years to get this idea, so hang in there. In the beginning I suggest you consciously choose good food before every meal and choose to exercise every day. Soon it will become second nature.

'you need to make intentional, positive choices about your lifestyle; every one will improve your health'

22

total body transformation total body transformation total body transformation total body transformation total body transformation total body transformatio

A couple of bad habits

When I was younger, I got into the habit of eating ginger biscuits at night in front of the television. Every night after a cup of tea, I'd tuck into a packet like there was no tomorrow. Just what I needed – a mountain of simple carbohydrates just before bed. When I analysed it, I quickly realised that it was because I'd got into the habit of *buying* them, and that led me into the habit of *eating* them because they were there. When I realised it was a habit, it was pretty simple to break it – I just didn't buy them, and if they weren't in the house, I couldn't eat them. It wasn't that hard – now I just have a cuppa. I don't even miss the bikkies any more.

I also had a friend who used to grab a thick shake on the way home from work every night, and he pretty quickly came to the realisation that it wasn't helping him with his goal to lose weight (for the record, thick-shake addicts, this represents around 530 calories, approximately 25 to 30 per cent of an adult male's daily intake and about 35 to 40 per cent of a female's. If you can't live without them then I suggest you cut out the middle man and pour them straight on your thighs . . .) So he changed the route that he drove home, saved himself a kazillion calories and actually felt pretty good about it. He couldn't believe how he'd let the habit develop in the first place. Habits, like rules, are made to be broken. And the best way to break them? Start doing the opposite.

recognise emotional eating

Over the years, I've learned that emotional eating is the downfall for many people who struggle with weight issues. It's what so many of us girls do when the world gets tough, and quite a few blokes do it too (although it usually involves vast quantities of beer!) The result is the same, though – thousands of calories and mountains of regret the next day. I know only too well that food can be used as an anaesthetic, an antidepressant, a toast for celebration, a time-filler, a control mechanism, a diversion – anything besides actually satisfying genuine hunger. And what's even more bizarre is that many of us have forgotten what hunger is, and what it really feels like.

The key is to identify emotional eating as it happens and so understand what triggers an eating binge. Then you will be better equipped to combat it before it kicks in.

Before you run to the pantry because you're feeling emotional, ask yourself:

1. Am I *really* hungry?
2. What am I feeling?
3. When was my last meal?
   (Was it three or four hours ago? Or three or four minutes ago?)

'without action, acceptance goes nowhere'

So, if the answers to the above questions tell you that you are in fact *not* hungry but are eating because you are bored/upset/unhappy, what are you going to do about it? Are you strong enough to simply say 'no', or will it take a bit more than that? You may have to pick yourself up and do something like:

- take a shower
- go for a walk
- call your mum
- have a cup of tea
- read a magazine

- clean out a cupboard/box room
- throw out all your old 'fat' clothes.
- Or here's a cracker: go and try on some of the clothes that you've just started to fit back into if you've lost a little weight. This is usually very motivating, but be warned — it will often send you straight out for a jog!

Grab your notebook again and make a list of 'things to do instead of eating'. Tear it out and stick it on the fridge. Add new things to your list as you cross others off.

But I just *have* to have it!

Some people who are self-confessed chocoholics have sworn to me that they absolutely *neeeeed* to have chocolate every day otherwise they just can't function. 'Oh, but I need it!'

Firstly, this is biochemically inaccurate. The body does not need chocolate to function. So, if the body doesn't need it, where does the need come from? It's in their head. When I ask them to go for just two days without it, I tend to get a lot of, 'Well, yeah. I know I can go without it, it's just that I don't want to.'

Aha! Now we're getting down to it! So I ask them, 'But if you can go without it, why haven't you?' This is about the time for some more intense questioning.

'Okay, let's go back to your priorities. You told me you want to be X kilograms lighter by Christmas, and fitter and healthier. Is that still the case? I'm not asking you to give up chocolate forever, just for two days.'

By not having chocolate for two days they are able to see that firstly they *can* do it and secondly by doing so they *take back control*. From these realisations come self-belief, which is incredibly powerful. Show me someone who believes in themselves and I'll show you someone who can do *anything*!

everything, buy-one-get-one-free, more, more, more. Sure, you could argue that the food manufacturers should take some of the heat for this — after all, they're the ones that profit from our sugary binges. But ultimately it comes down to us. This food was not designed to be eaten this way, nor were our bodies designed to digest it in such huge volumes. And besides, we don't do victim, remember? **Blaming others for your poor choices belongs to the old you. Taking responsibility for yourself and making conscious choices that support your health and wellbeing is the new you.** See page 146 for more on portion control.

choose moderation

I have never been a believer in giving up all of my favourite foods or treats. It's just not realistic. It would leave you feeling deprived if you managed, or guilty if you didn't — a 'lose–lose' situation. Yet when it comes to food and alcohol, many of us find it hard to put on the brakes. In fact, some of us have even forgotten where the brake is. **We have lost the art of applying moderation and self-control.**

Some of us believe that 'moderation' means a *small* rather than a family-sized block of chocolate every day, and that 'self-control' is ordering a Diet Coke with our hot chips! Others have lost touch with the experience of enjoying some foods in the way they were designed to be enjoyed: sharing a small piece of cheesecake for a friend's birthday, or a chocolate treat once a week. Instead, there has been a mind shift to all-you-can-eat, king-sized

be consistent

Even after making our choice, human nature dictates that at times all of us will give in to temptation or allow ourselves a favourite treat. Perhaps we might skip a workout. This is life and we are all human, but it's how you handle yourself afterwards that's important. Maybe you had a special event scheduled and were going to have a couple of drinks that night and then get back in the saddle tomorrow. Or, maybe it just happened out of the blue. The key is consistency. It's about picking up where you left off and getting back on with it. Straight back to training the next day, or back to normal clean living. Let me tell you, I have had some of my best training sessions with a hangover.

Many of us fall into the 'all or nothing' approach where we use a momentary hiccup as an excuse to say, 'What the hell. I've ruined it now, I may as well just go for it' or 'What's the point in training? I missed two workouts so I may as well chuck it in.' It's another sneaky excuse, and a highly destructive one. Rather than telling ourselves that we're failures and going back to our old ways, the clever response is to say, 'Okay. I've had a momentary relapse into my *old* life. It was fun at the time, but it's not where I'm going, so now it's back to my usual routine — back to my *new* life.'

outmanoeuvre your weakness

Try this one on: self-control equals self-respect. **Respect your body by not filling it with garbage at every opportunity.**

For some of you it will take some careful and deliberate moves to make sure you don't end up with that tub of ice-cream in your lap, or the three family-sized chocolate bars that you bought when you were filling the car up with petrol. You need to 'outmanoeuvre' your weaknesses. Perhaps it means:

- Refuelling the car straight after you've had breakfast when you're not hungry
- Packing not one but two apples in your handbag so you're not tempted to go to a chip and soft-drink machine
- Eating a healthy meal before you do the grocery shopping
- Driving home a different way so that you are not going past those drive-through fast-food chains (better still, ride a bike or take the bus).

It's really about thinking ahead, knowing where you often slip up and taking the appropriate steps to avoid the pitfalls. Here are some other tips:

- Steer clear of food courts and go to the local sandwich shop instead where your choice is simpler. Then choose a healthy salad and chicken sandwich that'll be made right there in front of you.
- Have a healthy snack (such as a piece of fruit) before you go out to dinner if you know it's going to be a late meal. That way you are not diving into the bread basket when it finally arrives on the table. Better yet, ask the waiter not to bring the basket out, or have it moved to the other end of the table.
- Meet your friend for a power walk instead of a coffee and cake.
- Brush your teeth straight after dinner and then it's *game over*. If you're tempted, go for a walk (without your wallet or purse).
- Reward yourself with *anything* other than food. And that goes for your kids too.

the power of language

Your choice of words has a lot more clout than you may think, and this applies as much to your self-talk as it does to your dialogue with others.

Go, Greg!

Greg, one of the contestants on *The Biggest Loser*, was constantly beating himself up about how he had let himself go, worrying that his wife would leave him if he didn't clean up his act — unless he died from obesity-related health issues first. He was literally talking himself (and everyone around him) into it. Greg was also an athlete in his youth, and it killed him that he had let himself slip so far from the healthy young man he used to be.

But he took back control and began an aggressive weight-loss journey that saw him revert to his old athletic self, and with that came more positive language. Soon the 'can't' and the 'too tired' were replaced by the 'I can' and even the 'Get the hell out my way because I'm coming through!'

He not only fired himself up, but also the rest of the team. Interestingly, as his self-confidence returned, people really loved to be around him, including me. His positive outlook was infectious and soon he had the crew hanging out with him. Everyone loves being around positive, uplifting people!

Have you ever heard an Olympian speak about their goals or a mountaineer interviewed before a major climb? Their language reflects their belief in themselves. It's positive and productive, and it's a skill that has taken them time to learn.

Negative self-talk is a habit that forms like any other unproductive habit. When did it start? Who knows! But I bet you didn't tell yourself you were a stupid, fat cow when you were a five-year-old. Back then I bet you thought you were invincible and ready to tackle the world! Granted, the world back then was kindergarten, but it doesn't matter because it was *your* world.

Take the time to stop and listen to what you are saying, even when you think it's an off-the-cuff comment. We are so used to putting ourselves down that we don't even notice a put-down any more. **Particularly watch out for humour that disguises self-loathing,** in comments such as: 'I might be a big guy, but there's a whole lot more of me to love' or 'Look out! Big sista comin' through!'

I once had a client whose email address was bigfatgirl@whatever.com — I'm not kidding. I had her change it immediately. She wasn't going to continually put it out to the universe that she was a big fat girl any more.

How often do you hear 'Oh, once I start eating I just can't stop. That's just the way I am.' That's crap, and you know it! That's you giving yourself permission to avoid taking responsibility for yourself and you've said it so many times you think it's true. Grow up! That sentence and any others like it are now *gone*.

total body transformation total body transformation total body transformation total body transformation total body transformation total body transformatio

My mate Craig was constantly picking me up when I used the word 'hopefully'. He would say to me, 'There is no hope!' which would have me thinking, *Well there's bloody confidence for you!* I always had him pegged as a positive kind of guy, which of course he absolutely is. He's the *most* amazingly positive person I know. Craig explained his thoughts to me about hope.

'How is what you're saying you *want* to happen *going* to happen if you are only *hoping* it will happen? What has hoping got to do with anything? Okay, I am really, really, *really* hoping now, Mishy,' and he would screw up his brow and try to stop giggling at the same time. Naturally I would slap him and tell him to shut up and stop being so right all the time.

How true is that, though? How many times do you hear yourself or others say: 'hopefully I'll be able to fit into those jeans by Christmas' or 'hopefully I will be able to get fit and lose weight by summer'.

Yeah, and I'm hoping for world peace! Take 'hope' out of your vocabulary and replace it with words denoting action, not aspiration. 'I **will be** a kilo lighter by the end of this week' instead of 'I **hope** I lose a kilo this week'.

I reckon we do it as a backstop. 'I'll use the word hope, just in case I fail and then I can say that I didn't really mind either way.'

And while we're here, why are we so hung up on failure? I hate failing. It totally sucks. But I have learned some major lessons through my failures, lessons that have made me more

determined. Lessons I wouldn't have learned if I had succeeded. Not achieving what I set out to do certainly didn't kill me and it made me appreciate achievement so much more.

At some point you've just got to go for it and say, 'I am going to do this! And no minor setback is going to stop me.' You must absolutely stand up and shout it to the world, that you're like a heat-seeking missile homing in on your destination. This is the attitude of people who achieve their goals. This is truly the path to success.

stop living off past glories

If you played sport in your youth, you learned about working with others towards a common goal, about respecting the rules, about commitment, discipline and of course about yourself. I honour those individuals who 'got into it' during their childhood and teenage years.

People with athletic backgrounds are often well placed to make dramatic gains in weight management as they are no stranger to intense exercise and it's almost as if their bodies 'remember' the way they were, making the journey back easier. The flipside, though, is that they sometimes talk up how fit they *used* to be, how amazing they *were* at football/swimming/rowing or whatever so that we won't notice they're not at their best today.

I'm not saying they shouldn't be proud of their past achievements, just that they should not use them as an excuse for their current situation. For some, I also get the sense that they

Barefoot Bernie

Bernie is a friend of mine, and every time I see him he blows me away. He's eighty-two years old and trains five to six days a week. He does a bit of everything: weights, boxing, martial arts and barefoot waterskiing. Yes, that's right, folks, *barefoot*! He is fit, agile and looks about twenty or thirty years younger! Bernie is truly amazing. But here's the thing: we can all be amazing. He is no different to anyone else, and like the rest of us he wants to live a long, happy life. He has taken care of his body all his life and has the utmost respect for it. And the prize for this? A rich life full of action and fun right up to his eighties and beyond. It is possible.

cannot handle the stark reminder of just how far they've let themselves go. It's as if they're saying, 'If I can't be the best, I won't enter the race.' It's a mix of fear and ego. Now there's nothing wrong with a bit of ego, but that's ego in its most destructive form. And it's nuts! Think about it. What you're doing is refusing to participate because you don't want to face not being the best, not being the winner. Would you let your children get away with that kind of attitude? I doubt it! And wouldn't you tell them that it's not about winning, it's about 'playing the game', about participating? **Because let me tell you, everyone who is having a go is a winner.** That's right, the big girl up the back of the group fitness class — WINNER!

The old bloke struggling through a yoga posture — WINNER! The wheezing mums pushing prams up a hill at 6 a.m. — WINNERS! These people are the source of my inspiration.

I have the answer to the 'past glory' non-participators. *So what!* Who cares? So you used to be in the school footy team? Great, at least you know what hard training is about. So you used to weigh 140 kilograms, but you dropped to 110 five years ago? Great effort, but it doesn't stop there. You can't hang your hat on that and hope to get away with it. If you're fifteen or twenty years older now and still languishing in the glory of being a seventeen-year-old *you're dreaming*. **That was the past — this is the present — so let's get *moving*.**

'if you want to impress me, be the best you can be at the age you are now'

4
you gotta have a plan,man!

'it's knowing how you're going to get there that makes it happen'

EVERY GREAT JOURNEY NEEDS A MAP. The best navigators are the ones who have considered all the parts of the journey. They take into account fuel, terrain, weather, equipment and other factors such as communication in emergencies.

It's the same for you on your weight-loss journey. If you are serious about making this happen, you need a game plan. And it's got to be realistic — by this I mean that you must **acknowledge what you've got and how you can make the best of it.** In other words, if you are small and heavy, you will not be able to get your body to look like something off the catwalk.

It's a pretty tough call, particularly when we are bombarded with images of what 'perfect'

women and men are supposed to look like. To some degree we are seeing a move away from this thinking, with role models who refuse to fall into line, who are happy with their bodies the way they are. But it's hard not to be weight-obsessed with media headlines like 'Celebs' Fat Days', 'Celebs' Beach Bodies', 'Detox in Three Days', 'Seven Days to Washboard Abs' . . .

It's endless, and we *all* know it's bullshit, but we still let ourselves get sucked in. So get past aiming for the unachievable and just take these images for what they are — digitally altered pictures of pretty boys and girls who have just as many bad hair days as we do.

Earlier on I spoke about how we tend to hate our body when we're struggling with our weight, and how we must accept, embrace and love our body because it's perfect as it is. You won't be able to move forward on your journey until you take this important step, so if you've been hating yourself, picking at your imperfections, beating yourself up about how you look, it's time to do the opposite and **start loving your body because it's your body, and it's the only one you've got.**

Think of it like this: you've hated your body for a while now, but has it helped? What if you did the opposite and started giving it a little love? I have all my clients say out loud 'I love myself and I love my body.' I get them to say it to me until they *believe* it. I talk more about this in Chapter 5.

set your goal

The next step is to ask yourself what you really want. What is it that you are looking for? What is the life-changing result that you want to achieve? Is it only about weight loss? Or is it about fitness too? Do you have some health issue that must be addressed, such as high cholesterol or high blood sugar levels? You need to be absolutely clear about your plan. And as with all plans, it needs to be **SMART:**

S   SPECIFIC — no fluffy stuff — be crystal clear about where you're going. For example, 'I'm joining a gym today.'

M   MEASURABLE — get all the cold, hard numbers so you can monitor your progress: get on the scales, take your measurements, try on your skinny clothes, calculate your BMI (see page 46), see your doctor and get your blood pressure and cholesterol readings.

A   ACHIEVABLE — your goal needs to be one that you are capable of reaching given your available time, job and family commitments, etc.

R   REALISTIC — similar to achievable, but a notch higher. For example, 'I'm going to lose 20 kilograms in the next twelve weeks' is realistic (especially if you are morbidly obese) but 'I'm going to lose 20 kilograms in the next three weeks' is not, unless you plan to lose a leg in an unfortunate shark attack.

T   TIME-BASED — once you've set your goal weight, then you need to draw up a day-by-day, week-by-week plan and execute it with precision. For example, 'I will lose 20 kilograms in twelve weeks, which is 1.5 kilograms per week.'

Now that you have a clear understanding of what you are aiming for, it's time to go get it!

1. get on the scales

Yep. That's right, you heard me. And if you don't have any, go and buy some good ones and then come back to this spot. Your scales and tape measure are your tools of the trade because they're how you'll measure your success.

Take out your notebook and write down your weight, the day and the time. You will weigh yourself at the end of each week at the same time.

2. get out the tape measure

You'll notice that the words 'want' and 'try' don't get used in the SMART terminology. 'I want to lose 20 kilograms' means just that — you want to lose 20 kilograms. 'I'm going to lose 20 kilograms' means just that — you *will* lose 20 kilograms.

Measure your chest, waist, hips, thighs and arms. Try to be accurate and also record your methods of measuring. It's *really* important to do it the same way each time, so if you have someone helping you, try to use them again.

- **CHEST:** girls, run the tape measure right across your nipples with your bra on. (Boys, you can take your bra off!)
- **WAIST:** use your belly button as a guide.
- **HIPS:** measure your hips at the widest point.
- **THIGHS:** measure the distance from the tip of your pelvic bone (iliac crest) down to the side of the knee joint. Halve the distance and mark that point on your leg with a pen. Now, wrap the tape around the mark. Do the same on the other leg.
- **ARMS:** measure from the tip of the shoulder joint down to the elbow. Halve the distance, and draw a mark. Now wrap the tape around the mark to measure. Do the same on the other arm.

'we can all talk about losing weight and exercising, but nothing happens until we actually do it!'

Now measure your height, and along with your weight calculate your body mass index (BMI) — see page 46. This will give you a handle on where your weight *should* be.

3. take a photo of yourself

Now get a pair of jeans, preferably ones that are hard to do up. Then choose a non-stretch shirt or top that you're struggling to get into. These are your 'benchmark clothes' and often work better as motivators than measurements. Take a photo of yourself in them, and then take one of yourself in your underwear or swimmers. (If you're sweating on this, just remember that I ask all my 12 Week Body Transformation participants to post their photos online!)

4. get a calorie counter

You'll need it when you get to the end of this chapter. Make sure it's an *Australian* one. Don't waste your precious time with some American or English publication (just what the hell is an aubergine anyway?) And don't bother complaining to me that calorie counting is no good — **you absolutely have to know how much fuel you're taking on board just as much as you need to know how much fuel you're burning.** I mean, if you were going to drive interstate would you really do it without knowing how much petrol you have in the tank? Of course not! This journey is no different.

'But you can't expect me to remember all those numbers,' I hear you say. Just check in on what you usually eat — we're creatures of habit so there's usually only a dozen or so foods that we habitually buy — it's really not that complicated. And besides, weren't you the one saying, 'I really want this! I really want to lose weight! And I'll do whatever it takes!'?

5. make a calendar

Put together a large calendar and stick it up where you see it every day. **Mark on it your target weight week by week, month by month, until you reach your goal weight.** (See Chapter 5 for how to calculate your healthy body weight.) So if you're going to lose 24 kilograms in twelve weeks then your weight needs to be coming down by 2 kilograms per week.

But is this realistic? In my experience if you weigh 130 kilograms or more you can expect to lose between 1.5 and 5 kilograms per week, with the first few weeks showing the greatest losses. (One of my clients who weighed 165 kilograms lost 6.5 kilograms in the first week!)

If your weight ranges from 100 to 129 kilograms you can lose around 1.5–3 kilos per week, or if you are under 100 kilograms you'll usually drop between 0.5 and 1.5 kilos per

week. Of course, much of this will depend on your commitment and determination, which will be tested when you have a week where you did not lose as much as you planned. Just *keep going* and re-read 'Be consistent' on page 26.

YOUR WEIGHT	EXPECTED WEIGHT LOSS PER WEEK
less than 100 kg	0.5–1.5 kg
100–129 kg	1.5–3 kg
more than 130 kg	1.5–5 kg

6. plan your daily workout time

Okay, this is the *big* one! This is the key to reaching the target weights you've marked on your calendar. It's time to go through your diary because it's critical that you find the time to exercise. (See 'Get Moving' for all you need to know about your workouts.) Before you open your mouth, don't give me the old 'I don't have enough time'. That's crap and you know it. **If you've chosen to do this, this is the work you must do to make that change a reality.** Maybe you need to be setting the alarm earlier. Morning training is not only great for being uninterrupted, but is also biochemically better for weight loss because your glycogen stores are depleted and your body *has* to source other energy sources (fat).

Once you've assigned your training time, book it in as an 'appointment'. Then when someone is trying to pull you out of it you can tell them, 'Sorry, I have an appointment between 1 and 2 p.m., but I can see you after that.' People aren't likely to ask you what kind of appointment you have, and if you tell them it's a workout they will usually try to tell you that it's not that important, that you can just skip one, that you don't need to train, blah, blah, blah. They will project their own guilt about not exercising on to you, and remember — we're not having negative people around us. So simply tell them that you have an appointment — it'll save a lot of time *and* will guarantee you get to your workout.

Be realistic about your time. If your job has got you behind your desk until 7 p.m., then you may have to restructure your day so you can exercise either early in the morning or at lunchtime. Or, put it to your boss that you will start earlier on the days that you want to leave earlier. If you have children, organise childcare with the school, your partner or family/friends. Or find a gym with a crèche if you have a pre-schooler.

'your body is the perfect piece of machinery: when you feed it well and exercise it regularly, it will respond perfectly and stay trim and healthy'

outlook and ultimately to your relationship with them. You need to blow them away with your honesty, courage, determination and spirit, which will happen naturally if you speak from the heart. This conversation has three critical elements:

- You will be declaring to the people who are important to you that you are tidying up your physical and emotional wellbeing.
- You are enrolling those around you in your plans, helping to ensure your success.
- You are exposing yourself to the potential of a breakdown and therefore a breakthrough.

7. get support

It's vital to have a network of close **family and friends** who are fully aware how important this is to you, and who will support you. This step must not be missed. You absolutely must have an 'enrolment conversation' with them. Make a time to get together with your closest family members where there will be no distractions. Call it a 'family meeting', and make sure you have their full attention (no TV on in the background etc.).

This is where you are going to inspire them with your passion so that they can help you make the positive and fulfilling changes to your health, your body, your fitness, your

Be brave! Go over the changes that you need to make with them — the exercise, the going to bed earlier so you can train in the mornings, the changes in the food that you'll be eating. Your passion will be infectious and you may find others around you will want to join you in your goals. But whether they accept or reject your plan, welcome or disapprove of it, ultimately doesn't matter. This is about YOU.

My guess is that you'll probably be greeted with *shock* (especially if you are someone who never speaks about their weight), *tears* (it might be the first time you've got real with your family

'set yourself goals — we grow and improve as people by striving to meet challenges and testing our abilities'

in a long time) and *respect* because ultimately they love you. **The bigger the emotions, the better!**

Make an appointment to **see your doctor** for a full check-up — you'll need to record your vital stats (blood pressure, cholesterol level). I talk more about this on page 63.

8. throw out all the crap food in your house

Get rid of all the sugary, processed foods in your pantry, fridge and freezer. If you're not sure what has to go, have a look at Chapter 11. Then turn to Chapter 12 and copy down my fridge, freezer and pantry shopping lists and go shopping. (Make sure you have had a healthy meal before you hit the supermarket!) This is another reason why you need to have the enrolment conversation with the rest of your family, as you're less likely to get any bitching about what will no longer be found in the pantry. If the kids complain, remember that *you* are the adult. They can have what they want when they move out of home, get a job and pay their own way. Besides, as a parent it's your responsibility to have your children make the best possible start in the world, with healthy bodies, well-functioning brains and a strong sense of self — not overweight, self-conscious, embarrassed and facing a future with poor health and all the unhappiness and heartache that comes with it. **Setting up good nutritional habits is one of the best gifts you can give your children.** This is the *new* you — now you're in control; now you're in charge.

9. get a 'new you' journal

This is a journal I use with my clients to keep the plan going and to keep them on track. What does **NEW** stand for?

N   NUTRITION — you'll write down everything you eat and drink. Be descriptive: white, wholemeal, full cream, low-fat, etc. Write down the calories and add them up at the end of each day and each week.

E   EMOTION — you'll record how you are feeling emotionally each day. How did you feel when you woke up? Were you lethargic all day? Were you on fire all day? What was your 'self-talk'?

W   WORKOUT — you will fill in the details around not only your formal training session and how you felt during it, but any incidental exercise you did as well. This is where you will log how many calories you blew off in your training sessions (see page 51).

This journal is your bible. It is the tangible reference to each step you take towards your goal. It is where you learn about your exercise: what's working, what isn't, where you train better — inside or outside, morning or evening — and how many calories you can burn in one session. It's where you learn about your calorie intake: are you eating too little during the day and too much at night? It's also where you learn about yourself, and how these changes are affecting you mentally and emotionally. Use the 'new you' template on pages 229–30.

10. start a seven-day food diary

The first entry in your journal will be your measurements, followed by your Seven-Day Food Diary. You must write down *everything* you eat and drink over a week. The descriptions of the food and the quantities need to be very detailed. For example: white, brown or multigrain bread; full cream or soy milk; 1 cup of cooked brown rice; 250 ml low-fat milk coffee, etc. (See Richard's story on page 72 for an example page in an *honest* Seven-Day Food Diary.) The time of day that you have the food or drink is important too, so be accurate, and ideally have the diary with you all the time and fill it in as you go. **Most importantly, do not diet! Just eat and drink what you normally do.** This is crucial. As much as you might want to jump straight into a new healthy way of eating, believe it or not I must stop you. Trust me on this. You, my friend, must

understand *why* you are in this mess in the first place. **We learn nothing if we don't know why.** And isn't that your current mantra? 'I don't know why I can't lose weight'? *An accurate and honest diary of what you're eating is the first step!*

Using your calorie counter, work out your total calories for each day and the total for the week. Now you can look at the choices you have been making and decide what needs to change.

- Are you skipping breakfast?
- Are you eating late?
- Are you bingeing at night?
- Are your portion sizes on a par with those of a 2-metre-tall lumberjack?
- Do you eat highly processed, sugary food (chocolate, chips, cake) every day?
- Do you avoid green leafy vegetables?
- Are you drinking alcohol most nights?
- Are you eating out a lot?

The telltale component to all this will be when you add up your calorie intake for the week. If you've been completely honest and not altered your eating habits it should now be no secret why you are overweight. (By simply cutting out biscuits, cakes, sweets and chocolates and drinking low-fat milk; you'd see an *amazing* difference over several weeks, even if you didn't exercise!)

You need to continue keeping the food diary in your journal, adding up the calories, until you reach your goal weight.

get *moving!*

5

body
basics

*'you can't move forward if you
are in a state of self-loathing'*

I KNOW, I KNOW – YOU'VE HEARD IT ALL BEFORE: being sexy has more to do with attitude than with looks. But have you really stopped and listened? Have you truly allowed yourself to believe that you are perfect just the way you are? As I said in the 'Get Real' section, accepting yourself is a vital step that you must take before you start your weight-loss journey. Your body is uniquely yours, no one else owns it, and you can't move forward if you are in a state of self-loathing. Only when you love something can you truly take care of it, and right now by reading this book, that's exactly what you're doing: committing to taking care of yourself.

Still, you'll need to work with what you've been given. If you are dreaming of looking like a catwalk model and you're a stocky 150 centimetres tall, then you may as well turn the boat around and start rowing in the opposite direction. If, however, you want to keep rowing to Catwalk Island, then you'd better find yourself another captain, because I'm sure as hell not wasting my time or yours trying to get you there. You do need to dream big when you are setting goals for yourself, but remember the 'R' in our SMART objectives, and keep it *real*.

body types

Understanding a few basic principles about body types can help you appreciate your own body, and understand how best to train and feed it. People are commonly described as being ectomorphic, mesomorphic or endomorphic, and while I'm not one for technical medical terms, they're useful descriptions.

Most of us are combinations of these body types. By way of example, there aren't many pure mesomorphs out there, but there are plenty of mesomorphs with ectomorphic or endomorphic traits.

Your body type will have a significant influence on your physical potential, and you need to accept that. For example, if you are a woman around 1.6 metres tall, weigh over 90 kilograms, have struggled with your weight all your life and tend to hold weight around your stomach and breasts, chances are you are an endomorph. There is *plenty* we can do to help you. However, if your goal weight is to be a size 10 you will have to get real and accept your natural body shape. So let's aim for a size 12 to 14 with toned muscles and take it from there, huh?

ECTOMORPHS are naturally thin. They tend to have fast metabolisms (in other words, their bodies use up energy/calories quickly) and they need food regularly or else they get cranky, and they can usually eat lots of food without putting on weight. When ectomorphs put on weight, they tend to put it on around their hips, thighs and tummies.

MESOMORPHS are more like the classic Grecian-statue type — broad shoulders, narrow waist, with evenly distributed body fat. When trying to lose weight these people don't tend to have 'stubborn spots' and their bodies respond very well to training.

ENDOMORPHS tend to have slower metabolisms and put on weight easily, particularly around the stomach.

body mass index

Body mass index (BMI) is a widely used indicator to classify an individual's weight status. It's probably not the best indicator of health risk (your waist measurement is better — see page 47), but it's a pretty useful tool to work out your weight-loss goal.

Your BMI is calculated by dividing your weight by your height in metres squared. So, if you're 1.55 metres tall, and you weigh 78 kilograms, your BMI will be:

$$78 \div (1.55 \times 1.55) = 32.5.$$

If you don't have a calculator, use the table below or the BMI calculator on my website, michellebridges.com.au.

								BODY WEIGHT (KG)									
147	41	44	45	48	50	52	54	56	59	61	63	65	67	69	72	73	76
150	43	45	47	49	52	54	56	58	60	63	65	67	69	72	74	76	78
152	44	46	49	51	54	56	58	60	63	65	67	69	72	74	76	79	81
155	45	48	50	53	55	58	50	62	65	67	69	72	74	77	79	82	84
157	47	49	52	54	57	59	62	64	67	69	72	74	77	79	82	84	87
160	49	51	54	56	59	61	64	66	69	72	74	77	79	82	84	87	89
163	50	53	55	58	61	63	66	68	71	74	77	79	82	84	87	89	93
165	52	54	57	60	63	65	68	71	73	77	79	82	84	87	90	93	95
168	54	56	59	62	64	67	70	73	76	78	81	84	87	90	93	95	98
170	55	58	61	63	66	69	72	75	78	81	84	87	90	93	96	98	101
173	57	59	63	65	68	72	74	78	80	83	86	89	92	95	98	101	104
175	58	61	64	68	70	73	77	80	83	86	89	92	95	98	101	104	107
178	60	63	66	69	73	76	79	82	85	88	92	95	98	101	104	107	110
180	62	65	68	71	74	78	81	84	88	91	94	98	101	104	107	110	113
183	63	67	70	73	77	80	83	87	90	93	97	100	103	107	110	113	117
185	65	68	72	75	79	83	86	89	93	96	99	103	107	110	113	117	120
188	67	70	74	78	81	84	88	92	95	99	102	106	109	113	116	120	123
191	69	73	76	80	83	87	91	94	98	102	105	109	112	116	120	123	127
193	71	74	78	82	86	89	93	97	100	104	108	112	115	119	123	127	130
	19	20	21	22	23	24	25	26	27	28	29	30	31	32	33	34	35

HEIGHT (CM) *(row labels, left)*

BODY MASS INDEX (BMI)

Source: Deakin University 2006

Here's how the classifications look:

- **Less than 18:** very underweight, you may be malnourished
- **Less than 20:** slightly underweight, a good feed wouldn't go astray
- **20 to 25:** a healthy weight
- **26 to 30:** overweight — time to get moving!
- **Over 30:** obese — the party's over, major lifestyle changes coming your way
- **Over 35:** severely obese — you must act now to get your life back
- **Over 40:** morbidly obese — your weight is profoundly affecting the number of years you'll be on the planet complaining about it

Remember that these ratings apply to young and middle-aged adults. They aren't designed for the elderly or for children. Aboriginal people, Torres Strait Islanders and Asians generally have lower ranges due to their build, and the health risk may increase with a BMI as low as 23.

Note, too, that as you lose weight your BMI will drop, so you will need to recalculate it every few weeks. Also, BMI ratings don't apply to athletes who carry a lot of muscle — e.g. bodybuilders or people who regularly train with weights. Their BMIs will show them to be overweight or even obese!

waist measurement

While the BMI is a useful indicator of whether or not someone is overweight, research is showing that waist circumference is probably a better risk indicator of Australia's Number One killer — heart disease. And interestingly, fat deposits around the waist seem to be more dangerous for women than for men.

You should have recorded this measurement in the 'Get Real' section and written it in your journal, so go back and check it against this table.

Waist measurement is important because while you want to look good, you want to look good for *longer*. Keep an eye on this measurement — make sure you take it the same way each time.

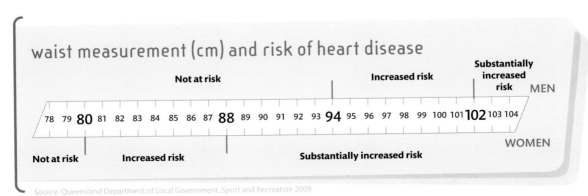

waist measurement (cm) and risk of heart disease

Source: Queensland Department of Local Government, Sport and Recreation 2008

6

calories in, calories out

'the higher your heart rate, the more calories you smash up'

OKAY. YOU KNOW YOUR GOAL WEIGHT, and you have planned the number of kilos you want to drop each week. Now we get down to the gritty stuff. Physically, your ability to gain or lose weight is determined by how many calories you eat compared with how many calories you burn. **Eat more than you burn – you get fat. Burn more than you eat – you get thin. It's that simple.** Sure, there are lots of other determining micro-factors, but if you're in the market for some serious weight loss, that's all you need to know.

What leaps out at me when looking at calorie expenditure and exercise is just *how much* you have to do to blow off calories you've taken on with the odd eating misdemeanour.

For example, next time you enjoy just one beer and a packet of potato chips (a 375 ml beer is around 150 calories (630 kJ); 100 g packet of chips around 500 calories (2100 kJ)) you can look forward to an hour and 10 minutes of full-bore, gut-wrenching cycling to get rid of them! Fancy a cappuccino (100 calories/420 kJ) and an extra-large blueberry muffin (500 calories/2100 kJ)? Prepare yourself for a 60-minute nonstop jog!

On the face of it, this doesn't seem all that bad, but wash down a croissant or its equivalent with two or more cappuccinos every day of your working week, plus any other crap you might have in your diet, and it's easy to see why you are putting on weight. Add to this little or no exercise and you *will* be going up a clothing size each year, no doubt about it.

A daily snack like this for morning or afternoon tea will give you a calorie load of over 3000 calories in just one week — that's nearly *two days'* worth of calories you've just tacked onto your weekly allowance! That equates to a gross weight gain of almost 2 kilograms a month. That's around *20 kilograms a year*! Any lights coming on out there?

Since I've got you on the ropes, let me ruin your day even further with some more examples of the calories in-calories out equation as it applies to a working girl or boy in everyday life.

- 1 glass champagne = 90 cal (375 kJ) power walk 2 km = 90 cal (375 kJ)
- 1 large chocolate muffin = 500 cal (2100 kJ) medium-pace jog 6–7 km = 500 cal (2100 kJ)
- 1 monte carlo biscuit = 90 cal (375 kJ) run up 15 flights of stairs = 90 cal (375 kJ)

By the way, if you're a metric lover, feel free to use kilojoules — I'm an old-school girl and still like to use calories, but as long as you're counting what is going into, and 'out of', your body, the unit of measure doesn't matter. **For the record, 1 calorie equals 4.2 kilojoules, so multiply your calories by 4.2 to get kilojoules, and divide your kilojoules by 4.2 to get calories.**

The number of calories you can burn off on a walk or run varies from person to person, but I think you get what I'm saying here. One way or another, everything you put into your body will either be converted into energy to fuel movement, or converted to your butt size. *This is why people making poor food choices stay overweight even though they are training hard.* They fall for what I call the Reward Syndrome: 'I trained this morning so I can eat this muffin.' I talk more about this on page 66.

Keep in mind that overweight people will generally burn more calories than smaller people because the more out of shape you are the harder your heart must work. The higher your heart rate, the more calories you smash up. However, overweight and unfit individuals generally can't exercise with the same intensity as fitter, thinner people because they have to stop for frequent rests during the same period, which will reduce their overall calorie expenditure.

When you've got a basic understanding of the calorie content of the foods in your life, and what it takes to get rid of them, you are better equipped to organise yourself into a calorie-deficit lifestyle. This is why I want you to continue your food diary until you reach your goal weight.

Working out how many calories we eat is the easy bit — we can just look them up in a calorie counter. Working out how many calories we burn each day is a little trickier.

We first need to work out our basal metabolic rate (the calories we burn just being alive) and then add any calories we burn through exercise/training.

basal metabolic rate (BMR)

Our BMR describes the calories used to keep our body functioning every day — our lungs full of air, our heart beating, our digestive system going and so on. We burn these calories when we are literally just sitting around, sleeping or even if we are flat out in a coma. Our BMR is influenced by a number of factors including our gender, our age, the amount of muscle we carry and whether we live in a hot or a cold climate, to name just a few.

 The following equations allow you to calculate your BMR. If you haven't already done so, go and grab a calculator and work out your

BMR right now, then write the result in your journal. Or go to my website (michellebridges. com.au) and use the BMR calculator there.

$$66 + (13.75 \times \text{weight in kg})$$
$$+ (5 \times \text{height in cm}) - (6.76 \times \text{age in years})$$
$$= \text{b.m.r. for males}$$

$$655 + (9.46 \times \text{weight in kg})$$
$$+ (1.85 \times \text{height in cm}) - (4.48 \times \text{age in years})$$
$$= \text{b.m.r. for females}$$

Note: there is a slightly more complicated calculation you can make that takes into account the calories you burn in your daily work — but in my experience, people with weight issues usually lead a sedentary life, or their activity levels can vary greatly, so I tend not to use it. Working from the lowest common denominator — their BMR — means that **any extra daily exercise is a bonus** for my clients!

exercise expenditure

The next step is working out how many calories you burn up in a training session. If you're not doing any exercise you'll have nothing to add here.

If you are doing some form of training, your expenditure will vary depending on:

- The type of training
- Your weight
- Your age
- The intensity of your training
- The length of your training.

calorie expenditure chart for 60 minutes of training

exercise	body weight 70 kg	80 kg	90 kg	100 kg	110 kg	120 kg	130 kg
Walk (light)	245	280	315	350	385	420	455
Walk (brisk) 6.5 km/h	280	320	360	400	440	480	520
Slow jog 8 km/h	560	640	720	800	880	960	1040
Jog 10 km/h	805	920	1035	1150	1265	1380	1495
Swim laps	560	640	720	800	880	960	1040
Cycle 16–20 km/h	420	480	540	600	660	720	780
Cycle 20–22 km/h	700	800	900	1000	1100	1200	1300
Cycle class (high intensity)	735	840	945	1050	1155	1260	1365
Group fitness class (high energy)	490	560	630	700	770	840	910
Weights (light)	210	240	270	300	330	360	390
Weights (heavy)	420	480	540	600	660	720	780

The best way to know how many calories you're burning during exercise is by using a **heart-rate monitor**. These not only display your heart rate, but also the number of calories you have burnt, and they have the added benefit of being *unique* to you. In other words, your heart rate is being calculated by the same equipment every time. Heart-rate monitors on gym cardio equipment can vary from one piece to another, plus they aren't always that accurate. Buy, beg or borrow a heart-rate monitor and strap it on!

Personally, I *always* wear mine when I train. I love knowing how many calories I've chewed up by the end of a training session. In fact, I sometimes use that as part of my training.

'Okay, Mishy. You have to expend 600 calories before you can stop, no matter what!'

I also love watching my heart rate while I'm training, as it tells me when I need to wind it up a notch or two. Sometimes I use it as a timer when I'm resting and tell myself, 'Okay, Mishy, you can slow down until your heart rate drops to 140, then get back into it!'

If you don't have a heart-rate monitor, you can use the Calorie Expenditure Chart above to estimate how many calories you burn during exercise. Figures in the table are really just an estimate, but will help you understand the energy in–energy out equation, which is crucial to your weight-loss success.

'your body is built to move — so move it!'

You'll notice that *the heavier you are the more calories you'll burn*, which is why people carrying a lot of body fat often lose it quickly to start with. But as we know, heavy people are generally unfit and can't keep up the intensity in their training so their weight-loss often slows right down. The trick is to get fit as soon as you can so you'll get the best of both worlds.

My experience on *The Biggest Loser* reinforced this. Often contestants would rip up over 1000 calories in a 50-minute session! They were super-fit close to the end of the show even though they were still overweight, and their newfound fitness, coupled with an increase in their muscle mass, meant that they were blasting calories in their workouts and stripping body fat like crazy. Way to go!

So your simple weight-loss calculation will look like this:

basal metabolic rate + calorie expenditure
= calories burnt for the day

start counting

Okay, now that you know how many calories you're burning, you can work out if you're in calorie surplus or calorie deficit:

calories in – calories out
= calorie surplus or calorie deficit

To lose weight, you need to be in *calorie deficit*. In order to lose ½ kilogram per week you will need to be in deficit of around 3500 calories. Go back to your SMART objectives (page 33) and remind yourself how many kilos a week you need to lose to reach your goal.

Now grab your journal and calculate your required weekly calorie deficit. If you need to drop, say, 1 kilo each week, your calorie deficit needs to be around 7000 calories. Along with your food diary, you need to keep a daily tally of your calories in and calories out. (See page 229 for a template.) You absolutely *must* be committed to keeping your records. Here are a couple of examples to help you get started.

I first met Michelle when I was a contestant on *The Biggest Loser* in 2008. At the time I weighed 206 kilograms and was so unhappy. She guided me through an eye-opening regime of exercise and nutrition that has given me a completely new direction in life. When times were tough, Michelle encouraged me to believe in myself. Thanks to her, I now have a healthy diet and know how to train to get results. I have lost over 70 kilograms and am the fittest I've been since I was a kid. I'm also happier and more confident than I've been in over a decade. While it sounds like a cliché, it is oh so very, very true — I couldn't have done it without her.

Garry, 33

> *'we are surrounded by cheap, empty calories,*
> *but the power is in our hands to take back*
> *control over what we eat'*

Example: client 1

	calories in	BMR	workout	calorie surplus/ deficit
Monday	1290	1461	323	−494
Tuesday	1310	1461	468	−619
Wednesday	1385	1461	502	−578
Thursday	1280	1461	0	−181
Friday	1300	1461	545	−706
Saturday	1356	1461	0	−105
Sunday	1275	1461	200	−386
total	9196	10 227	2038	−3069

This client is just getting back into shape. She is 157 cm tall and weighs 72 kg, giving her a body mass index of 29 (see page 46 for an explanation of BMI), technically classifying her as overweight. She is thirty-seven years old, works in an office and her fitness is quite low. Her goal is to lose 13 kg.

I have set her daily intake at a limit of 1300 calories and asked her to train six out of seven days with one of the day's exercise being a fun bike ride with her family.

She managed to get all her workouts in except for one (Thursday) and did very well cutting her calorie intake. Being 3069 calories in deficit, she lost less than ½ kg in one week. Although her goal was to lose 1 kg in one week, she knew that if she hadn't missed that workout and had amped up her other training sessions, she would have made it. So this was a good lesson. But hey! She's stoked. She's got her head sorted and she feels better than she has in years. Plus, she knows where she's going and she knows she's going to get there. She's taken back control.

The key for her is not to miss her workouts. And right now, two out of the six workouts need to be 'gut busters', meaning she will need to tough it out either longer or harder (or both) to burn more calories.

Example: client 2

	calories in	BMR	workout	calorie surplus/deficit
Monday	1780	2234	1021	−1475
Tuesday	1630	2234	773	−1377
Wednesday	1700	2234	952	−1486
Thursday	1600	2234	910	−1544
Friday	1610	2234	1100	−1724
Saturday	3500	2234	898	−368
Sunday	1650	2234	0	−584
total	14 260	21 301	4289	7822

This guy is thirty-five years old, weighs 106 kg and is 189 cm tall. His basal metabolic rate works out at 2234. His goal is to lose 15 kg.

We started his daily calorie intake at 1700 and his training at one hour a day, five times a week. Two sessions were with me and three on his own. I asked him to be more active on day six and to rest on day seven. His treat meal is Saturday night. On Saturday he decided to do an extra workout so that he felt free to indulge, and he also made a conscious effort to increase his daily activity levels – taking the stairs, walking to meetings, etc.

By the end of the week on paper we had him pegged at just over 1 kg down. However, due to increased general activity levels (taking the stairs, etc.), the scales showed him as 2 kg down and he was thrilled. (Remember, the human body is not like a computer – hormones, stress and activity levels can throw out your careful calculations, often for the better. The key is to be consistent and stay on course.)

Because we had gone through smart food choices he did not feel hungry, and although he admitted that he occasionally thought about cheating, he waited for Saturday night, which he thoroughly enjoyed.

7
debunking
the
myths

'stop over-analysing it! put your joggers on and just get moving!'

BEING IN THE FITNESS INDUSTRY for as long as I have has exposed me to lots of useful information and experience, and also to a lot of crap. Let's see if we can clear the decks before we set sail . . .

myth 1: walking is a great way to get fit and lose weight

Using myself as an example, I know that if I power walk for 10 minutes along a flat road I'll burn around 20 calories, which is about the calorie content of a raw carrot. By comparison, if I run for 10 minutes on a flat road at about 10 km/h I will burn around 100 calories, which is a regular low-fat flat white coffee with no sugar.

Now, when the Number One excuse for not exercising is that we don't have enough time, I know which exercise routine I would rather devote my 10 minutes to. If you only have 30 minutes to dedicate to exercise, then passive exercise isn't really going to give you the results you are looking for, and frankly I categorise walking the dog or taking a morning walk with a girlfriend for a chat as 'passive exercise'.

In other words, if you want to lose weight at a reasonable rate, then forget walking because your calorie expenditure just isn't time-efficient. You'd need to walk at a brisk pace for 45 minutes just to burn off the coffee that you'd probably have afterwards, in which case the net benefit to your weight-loss goals would be *zero*.

There's nothing wrong with going for a walk. In fact, it's one of the best ways to clear your head, get some fresh air and lift your spirits. But if your goal is to burn off excess body fat and calories, then you'll probably find yourself becoming highly unmotivated because it's not going to get you the results you're after.

Having said that, we've all got to start somewhere and walking *is* a great place to start, but allow me to emphasise the word *start*. **You must be ready to push your boundaries at every session and never go back.** Your plan should be to graduate from walking to power walking, then timing your power walks and gradually upping the intensity so that you either walk further or walk the same distance in less time. From there you add some jogging along the way, and so on.

So don't whine to me that nothing is changing for you physically when your formal exercise program continues to be a casual stroll with your girlfriend. This kind of passive exercise is good because you're moving, but it's not what you should be spending a lot of time doing if you're trying to lose weight.

myth 2: low-intensity exercise burns more fat than high-intensity exercise

The argument here is that low-intensity exercise sources almost all of its energy from fat stores, which is true. This little charmer was put out by the equipment manufacturers to encourage more people to cruise around the cardio gear thinking they were burning fat because they were training at 65 per cent of their maximum heart rate while flicking through a copy of *Cosmopolitan*. Now, low-intensity exercise *does* chew into body fat, but you need to be there *a lot longer* to blow off a decent number of calories. And let's recall the Number One reason for *not* exercising? 'I don't have enough time.' So it's a no-brainer! Train smarter, harder and get the hell outta there! High-intensity exercise uses *bucket-loads* of energy and hence plenty of fat. *Plus*, the harder you train, the fitter you get; the fitter you get, the harder you can train and the more calories you can expend.

myth 3: never train on an empty stomach

Well, this one is the source of plenty of debate. When you haven't eaten for a while, such as first thing in the morning, your body is glycogen-depleted and you are more likely to use stored fat as an energy source.

If, though, you find you become light-headed and can't train as hard as you'd like, then don't blow the workout — eat a light snack half an hour beforehand. A piece of fruit is usually the best thing. Personally, I love training before brekkie.

myth 4: you shouldn't train with weights every day

Can anybody tell me why not? Sure, you need to give your body time to recover from a hard weight-training session (note the word 'hard'), but you can still train with weights every day if you are training specific parts of the body in each session. For example: legs on Monday, chest and biceps on Tuesday, back and triceps on Wednesday, and so on.

I get quizzed a lot about the risk of 'over-training', but I have to be honest with you on this one — Olympians, professional athletes, yes, they can be exposed to over-training. But the average overweight Australian? Ah . . . not many over-trainers there. Anyone asking me about over-training is usually looking for an excuse *not* to train.

If you're in a gym, the idea is to use a variety of workouts to keep up the interest level, or if you have a favourite, vary the intensity so you can do it day after day. (I show you how to set up your own workouts with minimal equipment in Chapter 10.) The key is to stick to your schedule no matter what. As soon as you miss a training session, it becomes easier to blow off the next one. Before you know it, three months have gone by and you have done nothing.

You'll need to be tough and work around injuries. If you've got blisters, strap them up

'nothing, but nothing, holds back the years like weight training'

and keep going. If you've pulled a muscle in your shoulder, train your lower body, and train it harder. Just *do not stop*.

myth 5: pilates, yoga and stretch classes are great for weight loss

Okay. Let me lay this on you. Pilates and stretch classes are fantastic for posture, strength, flexibility and mind–body connection. But for weight loss? *Shithouse.* The heart rate simply isn't elevated enough to burn calories at any significant rate. If you want to slip in a Pilates class to help with core strength, or a yoga session to improve your flexibility and quieten your mind that's fine, but if you want to lose weight, you're barking up the wrong tree pose.

myth 6: you can spot-reduce fat

I'm sick of answering this one. No, you can't. End of story. Next question?

myth 7: women get big if they train with weights

Um, last time I checked, us chicks were loaded up with a little thing called oestrogen, which makes it tough to build muscle mass. For that you need testosterone. So . . . no, this one's a fairytale. However, we can all change the shape of our bodies for the better with resistance training, which means that your muscles will become more defined, toned and shapely. I continually get women coming to me overjoyed with their physiques after I've put them on a weight program. Nothing, but nothing,

holds back the years like weight training. My mum trains with weights and she's *hot*!

There is so much information out there now that tells us about the benefits of weight training for both men and women that you'd have to be nuts not to do it. Eating and drinking too much garbage will make you big! Training with weights won't!

myth 8: i'm not a sweater

I haven't met a person for whom exercise doesn't work. In fact, it would be hard to name a chronic illness that doesn't benefit from some sort of exercise. As for not being a sweater, I can only say that I have seen people training who don't sweat and quite simply they aren't going hard enough! I trained one girl who didn't think she was a sweater, and guess what? She didn't think she was a puker either!

There are a billion books, articles and reports on exercise: when you should do it, how long you should do it for, what you should wear, who you should do it with and what house your star sign should be in for the best workout. They're all deflections! Most of them are constructed by people who are peddling the latest 'omigod' breakthrough in exercise, or worse, are trying to sell you something — pills, shakes, potions, wraps, you name it!

Everyone is just trying to make this harder than it actually is! Stop over-analysing it! Put your joggers on and **just get moving!**

8 enough talk, action!

'it's your mind that's got your body where it is today'

OKAY, YOU'RE PASSIONATELY COMMITTED TO becoming a leaner, fitter you, and you've worked out how to track your progress by measuring calories in versus calories out. Now you are going to *exercise*. That's right. **You will be an exerciser,** *forever*. Not just until you fit into that dress, or until your birthday or till you look great so you can dump your boyfriend while looking hot. No. You are an exerciser. Period.

Exercise is the fountain of youth. Research shows that it not only acts as a preventative, relieving you of the stresses and anxieties that can bring about illness, but that it also has amazing curative properties. Researchers at Duke University, for example, studied people

suffering from depression for four months and found that 60 per cent of the participants who exercised for just 30 minutes three times a week overcame their depression without anti-depressant medication.

Not only does exercise make you stronger, fitter and lighter, but you get to live a more pro-ductive and active life *for longer*. Not because you are on a cocktail of drugs and have to sit at your window with a rug over your lap and watch the world go by until you die. You get to be independent, healthy and fit, and probably end up carking it in a skiing accident at the age of ninety-three! And still a size 12!

Clearly, exercise does so much more than help you lose weight. It's actually unnatural for us *not* to exercise, and we are seeing the results of this with surging levels of obesity, mental illness, diabetes, heart disease and other illnesses that have evolved and multiplied as a result of our sedentary lifestyles.

we are designed to move!

If you look at the human body, it's designed to move. We have multiple moveable joints which allow us to do much more than sit on a couch.

Yet, here is an example of an everyday Australian's daily activity schedule:

1. Wake up
2. Sit down to eat breakfast (maybe)
3. Get in car and drive to work
4. Get in lift to get to office
5. Sit at desk
6. Eat lunch at desk
7. Get in lift to get back to car
8. Get home and sit down to dinner
9. Sit in front of TV
10. Get into bed

Next day — press repeat.

For a lot of us, this is a snapshot of our everyday lives, and it doesn't even take into account the health implications and weight issues that go with such a zero-movement lifestyle.

When it comes to our bodies, the old 'use it or lose it' mantra goes for everything – bones, muscles, heart, lungs and our brains. This fact is backed up by a multitude of research, but my favourite study was carried out by a bloke called R.N. Pavlou and his team in 1985. He got two groups of mildly overweight men and put them both on a rapid weight-loss diet for eight weeks. He also got one group doing aerobic exercise three times a week. The exercising group lost 11.8 kilograms in total, and the non-exercising group lost 9.2 kilograms. Not much difference, I hear you say. Except that of the 11.8 kilograms lost by the exercising group, a full 95 per cent of it was fat loss! This compares to only 64 per cent fat loss by the non-exercisers. The exercisers also looked better and were better equipped to keep losing weight because their metabolisms had elevated.

So, when you're stripping weight off yourself, hang on to the muscle, because you're gonna need it!

where to start

You are about to send your body into a state of shock. If you have never exercised, or even if you're a lapsed exerciser, your body is about to get the biggest wake-up call it's had in years. However, unlike your old self, who would punish your body by eating crap and being inactive, you're going to dish out tough love by *working* your body and working it hard.

Get the distinction: on the face of it, your old self would've been 'spoiling' your body by feeding it sugary garbage and deep-fried whatever, but in fact you were punishing it because you hated it. The term 'spoiling' is actually spot-on, because that's literally what you were doing — ruining it. Now, though, you love your

Don't stop, Louise!

My girlfriend Louise is built like a greyhound and is a perfect candidate for long-distance running, but unfortunately had never been particularly confident in her physical ability.

An academic, she'd never really done much running, but one day she decided she wanted to go out for a bit of a jog with me. We had planned to run about 5 kilometres, but we were barely into the first kilometre when she said she'd have to stop for a breather.

I said quietly, 'Why don't we just slow down a bit? We won't stop and walk but we'll just do a slow shuffle, enough to catch our breath. In fact it doesn't even matter if we shuffle slower than we could walk.'

Although she agreed, I could see that she wasn't happy about the idea. She definitely would have preferred to stop and walk. As we shuffled along, I explained to her that we were far better taking the pressure off and slowing down to a very controlled shuffle than walking. This is because once you stop, it's very hard to start again.

I also reminded her that she was not dying. She was breathing, her heart was beating, and she was still moving. She was too concerned with her discomfort to acknowledge that the puffing and panting, the tightening muscles, the sweating and the elevated heart rate were signs that her body was working exactly as it should do under those circumstances.

'A lot of this is in your head, Lou,' I assured her. 'Sure, it's a bit uncomfortable, but you're okay. There's nothing to be afraid of. Your body's working just fine.'

We ended up running the other 4 kilometres without stopping, and she was terrific! Exhausted, but terrific! Lou tells me now that this was a turning point for her. 'Mishy, I just wanted to stop, but when you said I could take the pressure off and just shuffle it felt less threatening. And even though I *thought* I couldn't run that far, somehow I did. When you reminded me that I wasn't dying and that a lot of it was in my head, that made total sense to me.'

She went on to explain that she never thought that she could be athletic and sporty because she wasn't fit and was just 'no good' at physical training. She explained that at a young age she'd convinced herself she was the academic, not the sporty type. 'I was pigeonholed, Mishy!' she remonstrated.

What a great result! Louise now actually enjoys her running – something that she never dreamed she would be able to do. And mostly because she had convinced herself that she couldn't. Now she even runs half marathons. Go, Louie!

body. You embrace, accept and revere it, and you do that by taking it to hell and back!

When I first train people I show them no mercy, and although their minds can quickly buckle and fall apart, their bodies don't. **So when you're telling yourself 'I can't do this, it's too hard', that's not your body talking. It's your mind.** And it's your mind that has got your body where it is today.

get a check-up

Before you start exercising you'll need to see your doctor for a check-up. People with certain illnesses or who are taking particular medications may have difficulty losing weight easily. They will need to approach my weight-loss program under their practitioner's supervision. Whatever your circumstances, tell your doctor that you're leaving this overweight, unhealthy body right there in the waiting room and that you will need their support. This journey is best taken with as much help as you can get, so if there's a lot of negative talk around, I recommend you flick Dr Do-Little and find a practitioner who's on the same page.

I see many people start off with the best of intentions, but then get sick a couple of weeks in. After that, the comeback is even harder than the first session and it all quickly falls apart. That's when I hear, 'Oh, I tried going to the gym but it didn't work for me', usually around the barbecue (another pork sausage,

anyone? Come on, they're only seven billion calories . . .)

People who haven't exercised in fifteen years will often get sick after the first few workouts because their bodies are so busy trying to repair themselves that their immune systems are compromised. You've got to understand that your body is going to be *screaming* for nutrients and rest to help it recover when you get started on your exercise program.

get plenty of rest

Go to bed half an hour earlier and if you're a poor sleeper (which you may well be if you're

'your training will inspire you to stay motivated'

overweight) take steps to improve your sleep quality. These steps can include:

- No stimulants after midday. This includes caffeine, soft drinks and chocolate — the last two help you to gain weight so should be ditched anyway. Oh, and did I mention cigarettes? Kick those suckers to the kerb.
- Invest in a good bed. If you're wrestling with your partner over mattress space all night, then get yourself a bigger one (bigger bed, that is — not a bigger partner).
- Make sure your bedroom is dark. If your curtains or blinds let light through, replace them with ones that don't.
- Try burning lavender oil in the bedroom to calm and soothe you (don't forget to blow out the tea-light candle before you go to sleep).
- Keep electromagnetic gadgetry out of the bedroom (no TVs or computers).

drink lots of water

Most of us just don't drink enough water. While training, you should be aiming for around 2 litres a day. Many people actually confuse thirst with hunger. If you think you're hungry long before you're due for your next meal, try drinking a large glass of water — it will often dampen hunger pangs. Everything functions better when you are well hydrated and if you've waited till you're thirsty you've waited too long. Your wee will let you know if you are hydrated or not. Have no fear if it's clear. It's all wrong if there's a strong pong!

eat regularly and well

Eat well (see 'Get Cooking') and take simple supplements (a multivitamin and mineral combo plus vitamin C). Avoid megavitamins — you don't need massive doses. Supplements should be taken with or immediately before or after food as this helps with their absorption.

A low-calorie diet can disrupt the balance of cholesterol and bile salts in your body, leading to the formation of **gallstones**. Bile is stored in the gall bladder until it's needed for metabolising fats. If it stays there too long — because there's no fat to break down — little 'stones' develop. Eating regularly and including some good fats in your diet will keep the gall bladder working and releasing bile into your digestive system. But before you reach for that chocolate bar, a couple of slices of Burgen pumpkin-seed bread will provide 6.5 grams of fat, with only 1 gram that is saturated, plus over 10 grams of protein. Caffeine and small quantities of mono-unsaturated fats such as flaxseed oil, sesame oil or olive oil will help to reduce the risks.

Even without dieting, if you are overweight you already have an increased risk of

'it's never too late to start making changes'

total body transformation total body transformation total body transformation total body transformation total body transformation total body transformatior

developing gallstones. Studies have shown that a woman with a BMI of 30 or more has double the risk of gallstones than a woman with a BMI of less than 25. Women are more likely to form gallstones than men, particularly if there's a history of gallstones in your family. I know, girls — just add it to periods and uncomfortable heels.

Studies conducted at Flinders University have shown that weight-loss candidates who lose more that 1.7 per cent of their body weight per week for extended periods are up to ten times more likely to develop gallstones, so if you experience rapidly increasing pain in your right upper abdomen that lasts between 30 minutes and a couple of hours, or pain between your shoulder blades or under your right shoulder, please see your doctor.

beware the reward syndrome

A lot of people who embark on an exercise program can fall into this trap: 'I trained today, therefore I can eat XYZ.' I can't begin to tell you the number of people I've seen year after year endlessly doing the classes and gym programs prescribed by their personal trainers, but for whom nothing has changed weight-wise. And it's not just gym-goers — I see the same thing happening with people who are exercising out-doors, jogging or whatever. I even see it with fitness professionals.

Then they corner me at a social gathering, with a schooner of beer in one hand, a party pie in the other, and proceed to quiz me about why they can't lose the weight! What they don't understand is that **when it comes to weight loss, it's about *everything* you put in your mouth, not just food but alcohol and soft drinks too.** With the reward syndrome, you'll take two steps forward, then two (or even three) steps backward, which can be really disheartening, especially when you think of all those hours of hard training that you've done. No doubt you'll be fitter, but a size 12 you won't be.

Move more, eat less.

Not move more, eat and drink more.

do more informal exercise

Going to the gym three times a week sounds pretty good. But three out of 112 waking hours is a drop in the ocean if you are sitting on your butt for the rest of the time. If **formal exercise**

'aerobic activity is your number one weight-loss weapon'

is training in the gym, jogging or playing sport, then **informal exercise** is taking the stairs, walking to work, bike riding on the weekend or working hard in the garden. **Formal exercise + informal exercise = results!**

find a training buddy

A training buddy can really help you stay focused — it doesn't matter if they're not as charged up as you. Share your goals with each other so that you stay honest, and when one of you tries to back out of a session, the other can say, 'Hang on! You said you wanted to be in a bikini by Christmas!'

aerobic training

There are three main forms of exercise — aerobic (also called cardio training), strength (aka weight training) and flexibility. If you want to make a positive impact on your health and wellbeing *any* one of these types of exercise will help you. But if you want to lose weight, you need to structure your exercise regime around the exercise that will make you lose weight *fast*. Typically, aerobic exercise (also referred to as cardio training as it lifts your heart rate) includes jogging, cycling, rowing and group fitness classes such as step or indoor cycling. In fact, it's pretty much any activity that gets you huffing and puffing. When you're training aerobically, you not only source energy from oxygen but from carbohydrates

and, you guessed it, fat. So aerobic activity is your *Number One weight-loss weapon*, which is why I recommend you get yourself a heart-rate monitor. This is your *fat burning meter*, and it also shows your calorie expenditure. The harder your heart is pumping, the more energy (and calories) you're burning.

'So why can't I just go for a run every day to lose the weight?' I hear you ask. Good question — here are the answers:

- If you've bought this book, there's a fair chance you're not someone who has the technique or stamina to get the results you want from running, especially if you are planning to drop more than 10 kilos (though by the time you finish my workout program you will be a mean machine!)
- The structure of a workout program keeps you focused and honest (you are more likely to blow off a training session if you think it's just a couple of laps around the block).
- The strength component (weights) of your training will transform your metabolism from a two-stroke to a V8 — you'll trash calories *way* faster.
- Having a range of fun and challenging exercises sparks your motivation and interest. (If you're bored, it's pretty easy to roll over and press the snooze button . . .)

'the way we live affects how long we live'

- Once your body becomes accustomed to one kind of aerobic exercise (in this case, running), your calorie burning will plateau and you won't be able to drop as much weight.
- My training program teaches you to be a *savvy exerciser* who can adapt their exercise to work around injuries and changed circumstances — these are skills you will have *for the rest of your life.*

As we've seen, intensity in exercise is *crucial* to getting the results you want and knowing your heart rate is a way of measuring how intensely you are exercising. You can also use it to push yourself to your desired intensity level. It's a bit like having a training partner or a mean cow like me yelling at you! Your workouts become more scientific, and you can really keep a close eye on *exactly* what's going on with your body while you're training — am I burning fat right now? How many calories have I nuked?

calculating your MHR

The heart rates you'll be aiming for in your workouts are usually expressed as a percentage of your maximum heart rate (MHR).

There are several ways to calculate your MHR, the most common way being to subtract your age from 220 — although this doesn't accurately apply to children, the elderly or the very fit; it's really only a guide.

Your heart rate determines the energy sources your body uses, so broadly speaking you're burning fat almost exclusively (but not much of it) at around 65 per cent of your MHR, and a much bigger combo of fat, carbs (in the form of glycogen) and oxygen at around 85 per cent of your MHR. For example, if you're thirty years old your MHR is 190, so 65 per cent of that is 124 beats per minute and 85 per cent is 162 BPM.

interval training

Interval training is where you train at, say, 65–70 per cent of your MHR but then periodically ramp it up to, say, 85 per cent for a short burst. In practical terms, it's like jogging around a football ground but then breaking into a sprint across each end. This kind of exercise really improves your fitness and is one of my faves.

Studies conducted at the University of New South Wales have shown just how effective interval training really is, partly because it releases catecholamines that literally help singe the fat from your backside. From an exerciser's point of view, if you're told that you have to go hell for leather for 30 seconds and then you'll get 30 seconds' rest, you're more likely to rise to the occasion. By contrast, if you are told to go at the same intensity for a full hour, you'd probably baulk at the proposition and get a new trainer.

circuit training

My programs are about teaching people what they can do without me, so when I get the opportunity to train *with* people I usually do some sort of crazy circuit training that's new and interesting for them.

A circuit is a series of 'stations' where you exercise for a specified time or perform a specified number of repetitions of an exercise. These can be strength-based stations, cardio-based stations, a mix of the two, all upper body, all lower body, or both. You can time how long it takes you to get through the lot and then try to beat your time, or you can sprint four lengths of the room before you go to the next station. The combinations are bound only by your imagination and repertoire of exercises. Sometimes when I train with a friend we take turns making up the next exercise so we never really know what the session will look like till it's over and we're both destroyed. It's perverse, I know, but we're freaks.

plyometrics

Plyometric exercises (or plyos, as I like to call them) are used by sports people to build explosive strength and stamina. They feature a lot of jumping, bounding, throwing and pushing. They work well with cardiovascular and weight training as they tend to help 'spike' your heart rate, and they get you very, very fit. These exercises are *hard*, and I usually include them in intermediate rather than beginners' programs, so there are only a couple in your workouts.

group fitness classes

Group fitness is sweeping the planet because, unlike the old days, when aerobics all got a bit complicated, modern classes have better-trained instructors and a wider range of class options. Apart from being fun, they have other benefits:

- You don't have to think about what you're going to do — simply turn up and let your instructor do the thinking for you.
- They are held at specific times, ensuring that you actually *do* your training.
- They are safe because there is always an instructor watching what you're doing.

> ## My mum rocks!
>
> My mum started training with weights at fifty-four. She'd *never* trained before. Part of the reason she started training was to help her manage a hip-replacement operation, which she was due to have. Through her weight training she was able to put off the operation for six years! She trained the day before the operation, and was back at the gym six weeks later. My mum is fitter, happier and looks better than she did in her late forties. You are *never* too old to make positive changes to your health and fitness!

- There is an enormous range of classes. Apart from the conventional 'aerobics classes' that began back in the eighties, there are now pre-choreographed classes that instructors learn. These are well researched, less complex and easier to participate in, particularly if you've never ventured into a group fitness class before.
- You don't need to buy any gear.

There are loads of classes out there, such as those by Les Mills International. I've been involved with them for over a decade and particularly like their BodyPump (weights), BodyBalance (passive) and BodyAttack (cardio) classes.

weight training

Strength training, weight training, resistance training (or whatever you want to call it) is generally not included in weight-loss programs because it sources carbohydrates for energy rather than fats. These carbohydrates have been converted into glycogen (a type of sugar), which is stored in your muscles and in your liver. Unused carbohydrates are stored on your butt.

However, strength training is invaluable in a weight-loss program if it is done properly, i.e. with sufficient speed and intensity to get your heart rate up. I get sick of seeing boofy boys with big chests and skinny legs meander through their weight workouts and then complain to their mates about the size of their beer guts. Show me a weight trainer who trains hard with urgency and intensity and I'll show you one lean rock star!

Training with weights has its own language. Exercises are usually performed in 'sets', with each set made up of a prescribed number of repetitions or 'reps'. For example, your workout may include three sets of sumo squats with a barbell, with each set consisting of twelve reps.

Because I know the value of strength training for weight loss, you'll notice that many of the workouts in this book include weights. Importantly, all of the weight exercises are set out in the form of 'super sets', where you perform two sets of different exercises without a

main muscle groups

biceps

deltoids

pectorals

abdominals

quadriceps

deltoids

triceps

latissimus dorsi

gluteals

hamstrings

calf muscles

rest in between. This will get your heart rate up, improve your strength and endurance and *trash* fat cells.

flexibility training

Flexibility training, or passive exercise, includes stretch classes, Pilates, yoga and the like. Passive exercise improves core strength, relaxation and flexibility, which is good for everyone (especially as we get older), but for weight loss? Unless you're smashing yourself in a crazy Iyengar yoga class, *forget it*.

One of my clients was only doing this type of training and couldn't work out why her butt was not getting any smaller. Couple that with her use of the 'reward syndrome' ('I have "trained" today so therefore I can have this half bottle of wine') and she was going backwards. I took out four of the five Pilates sessions she was doing a week (she kept one), replaced them with cardio, strength, indoor cycling and a step class, cleaned out her diet and she dropped 3 kilos in the first week! Yee-ha!

Richard

I met Richard on a treadmill. I was running on mine, and he was trying to walk on his, though the treadmill kept stalling. Sensing his frustration, I stopped and offered some help, which he gladly accepted. After a quick chat I learned that this was his second session at the gym. He'd joined a week before and was on a 'mission' to lose weight. 'I'd love to be able to run like you. Maybe in another lifetime!' was his throwaway line.

'Well, that attitude will get you nowhere!' I replied. 'I could have you running the City to Surf if you really wanted to; you just have to want it enough.'

I guess it was a bit cruel of me to throw down the gauntlet like that; I mean what else could he say but 'yes'? So we organised to start training the following week. In the meantime, his homework was to complete a Seven-Day Food Diary (while not dieting), and go to the doctor for a check-up. A week later we did the numbers, and the stats went like this:

age: 39 years, male
weight: 121.5 kg
height: 178 cm
waist measurement: 119.5 cm

weight classification: morbidly obese
BMR: 2363
blood pressure: 145/87 (dangerously high)

Then he showed me his diary. I won't list the whole thing, just a weekday and Saturday, but you'll get the idea:

TUESDAY		cal	kJ
7 a.m.	1 large latte full milk 2 sugars	250	1050
9 a.m.	wholemeal roll with 3 fried eggs & tomato sauce	470	1974
11 a.m.	1 large latte full milk 2 sugars	250	1050
1.30 p.m.	grilled fish, salad, small buttered roll, 2 glasses wine	710	2982
5 p.m.	1 large Freddo frog	200	840
5.30 p.m.	1 large latte full milk 2 sugars	250	1050
8.30 p.m.	1 large bowl veg soup	190	798
	1 large roll with butter	280	1176
	main size veal pasta	400	1680
	2 glasses red wine	200	840
	2 scoops gelato	200	840
	total:	3400	14280

SATURDAY		cal	kJ
8.30 a.m.	1 large latte full milk 2 sugars	250	1050
10 a.m.	2 poached eggs	146	613
	1 slice buttered toast	200	840
	3 slices bacon	390	1638
	tomato	20	84
	1 large latte full milk 2 sugars	250	1050
2 p.m.	1 packet chips (50 g)	260	1092
	sausage in bread × 2	300	1260
	6 beers (at the footy)	900	3780
7.30 p.m.	steak, large	300	1260
	salad	30	126
	½ slice chocolate cake	170	714
	3 glasses red wine	300	1260
	total:	3516	14767

Richard's total calories for the week were a gobsmacking 26 000 (109 200 kJ)! I was blown away. How was this man still functioning? How come he wasn't suffering some chronic ailment, like death?! He was scoffing vast quantities of calorie-dense foods, and all at the wrong times. And he'd only had one day without alcohol. No wonder he felt tired a lot and often had headaches and indigestion.

I rewrote his nutrition plan and put him on 1800–1900 calories (7560–7980 kJ) per day with a goal weight of 92 kg by the time the 14 km City to Surf run came up – that meant he had five months to drop 30 kg – tight, but doable.

Richard was scared, excited and pumped all at the same time. Perfect! He trained with me twice a week and did four sessions on his own, two of which were group fitness classes (indoor cycling and weight training). The other two sessions were a mix of weights and cardio. We set up his diary so it worked with his busy schedule and he trained early mornings or lunchtimes, as he often had to stay at work late.

We went through menus and I showed him how to order well eating out, and set up some non-negotiable rules, including five alcohol-free days per week, never going back for seconds, and breakfast every day. As for the rest of his nutrition, we gradually got him to a place where he was organised, feeling full and sticking to the plan. His doctor also prescribed medium-strength hypertension medication for his blood pressure.

At his first weigh-in (a week after he'd started) he'd lost an amazing 5.8 kg, and he was *stoked*! After one month he was down to 110.1 kg, and his hypertension medication was reduced to a low dosage. The second month was a little slower in the weight-loss stakes, but he was still losing weight *and* getting fitter. He even joined the gym's running club and found he was easily keeping up at beginner level. By the end of the third month he weighed in at 97.8 kg. He looked terrific and was running for 8 km nonstop! His next goal was the City to Surf; he had two months to train, and he trained *hard*. He was now off his blood-pressure medication (his blood pressure clocked in at a healthy 125/75). Inspired by his success, Richard's wife had also started losing weight and exercising too – a delight for both of them.

Richard ran the City to Surf nonstop, in just 1 hour 48 minutes – an incredible result. I was there to meet him at the finish line. He cried, I cried – soppy, I know, but this man had literally reinvented himself in just *twenty weeks*! Today, Richard weighs 90 kilos and trains five to six days a week. He loves his life.

9
exercises that work

'what really changes bodies is grunting and sweating!'

OKAY. HERE ARE THE EXERCISES that will change your life. You can do almost all of them at home, with minimal equipment. (For the ones that do use gym equipment, I note non-gym alternatives.) In the next chapter I combine them in your twelve-week workout program. First, though, I need to explain why weight training is as crucial to weight loss as your cardio workouts.

weight training rocks

Much of the weight lost with fad diets is water and muscle. Because muscle is your very own body fat–burning furnace, your weight-loss opportunities will be severely compromised without it. The less muscle you have, the lower your basal metabolic rate and the harder it is to burn the calories you ingest. Got it?

You'll need to use all the resources you can because your body will, in fact, conspire *against* you losing weight! This is because our bodies don't have an inbuilt level of fat that they try to maintain. **Fat levels are entirely guided by how much fat we** *habitually* **store in our bodies through our diet and lifestyle.** When we've been storing fat for a few years at a certain level, our bodies naturally develop all the nerves, hormones, capillaries and connective tissue to support it. When you start to change all this by losing weight, your body quickly slips into defensive mode because it thinks that it's under threat of starvation. Your metabolism will slow down, your appetite will increase and *your body will start trying to store more fat*. This is especially the case when you lose weight quickly, because even though you think you *gained* the weight quickly, you actually didn't. No, no, no. That backside of yours has been in the making for some time. Weight gain tends to take place over a period of years, so it's hard to sneak past your body's survival mechanisms when stripping off fat quickly.

I see a lot of people desperate to lose weight *wasting their time* with exercises that simply aren't suited to a weight-loss program.

To understand why, you need to appreciate the difference between compound and isolation exercises.

COMPOUND EXERCISES use more than one muscle group. Think about it — when you climb a set of stairs you:

1. raise your right leg, flex your ankle and plant it on the step (hello hip flexor, quads, tibialis)
2. push yourself up to the next step (say g'day to quadriceps, hamstrings, gluteals, calf muscles, abdominals, lower back muscles)
3. repeat for the left leg.

That simple motion has actually recruited over 50 per cent of your body's musculature. Now compare that to one of those ditsy seated abductor/adductor machines, which uses just *two* muscles! Which one do you think will fast-track you to 'hot momma'?

ISOLATION EXERCISES, on the other hand, do just that — they isolate a particular muscle so that you can work *only* that muscle. This is fine if you're a bodybuilder, if you're training for a sports-specific purpose or are undertaking rehabilitation training for a broken limb or whatever. But when you want to lose weight,

'the less muscle you have, the lower your basal metabolic rate and the harder it is to burn the calories you ingest'

you need to burn as many calories as you can in your workout, and the way to do that is to get as many muscles involved as possible.

All of the exercises that I give you will be compound exercises because they simply burn more calories. So if you're looking around the gym and see a personal trainer hovering over a weight-loss candidate doing some crazy one-legged circus act, look on in sympathy. Then get stuck into your compound exercises.

keep it simple

I'm frequently asked what exercises I do in my workouts and I'm here to tell you that I keep it very, very simple. For example, there are just four elements to my leg workouts: squats, lunges, step-ups and various forms of cardio training. For my upper body I use mainly chin-ups, push-ups, bench presses and shoulder presses. I incorporate variations to improve muscle tone and to avoid getting stale in my workouts, but that's pretty much it.

From the thousands of exercises available I have selected the ones that I have found to be the **most effective for weight loss and overall athletic fitness**. Basic exercises are usually the best because they have a proven track record and are easier to do. I have also selected exercises that can be done either in the gym where there's a full range of equipment, or at home with minimal equipment. I have provided an easier version and a harder

personal trainers

I totally recommend getting a personal trainer. Make sure you get someone who is going to kick your ass. And no baby excuses or whingeing from you. Have them coach you through the exercises I give you in this section of the book. Get them to show you how to do them safely and with intensity so that you know you are not wasting your time. Suck your trainer dry about technique, why the exercises are done that way and about safety. A good trainer should set you up so that ultimately you can go it alone.

I do, though, have a problem with personal trainers who pull out the old 'muscle weighs more than fat' when you get on the scales after three weeks of training and haven't lost any weight (or worse yet, put it on). Muscle does, in fact, weigh more than fat; however, an overweight unconditioned person will never put on muscle quicker than they will lose fat. So if this has happened then both of you need to take some responsibility and stop wasting each other's time. You need to clean up your diet and stop rewarding yourself with food, and your trainer needs to push you harder and ensure that you're training hard when you're on your own. You must meet each other halfway.

version for some. The harder version usually uses more than just body weight. And you *must* start upping the weight if you want to lose the weight. So *keep challenging yourself*!

Of course, I have omitted a lot of exercises. This book is for those who want to lose weight, burn calories and change their body shape, and that's exactly what these basic compound exercises do. It's not for bodybuilders.

you gotta train hard

The next thing we need to be clear about is intensity: when you train you must *train hard*. Watchers of *The Biggest Loser* will know just how hard those guys go, so use their efforts as a benchmark for your own. Intensity is the one thing just about everyone gets wrong. Half of the fitness industry is so busy dreaming up different programs and variations of exercises that they've forgotten that what really changes bodies is grunting and sweating!

Your heart rate will tell you how hard you're going. The first two weeks of training is simply about routine, about getting into the habit of building your fitness. In saying that, still shoot for around 65–70 per cent of your maximum heart rate (MHR). See page 68 for how to calculate your MHR.

The next step is to start ramping up your workouts with bursts of 85 per cent MHR. Once you're in the 70–80 per cent range, your cardio-vascular system is really starting to kick in.

warm up & stretch down

If you are going it alone — no gym, no personal trainer — then more power to you. Remember, though, that every workout deserves a good warm-up, which can be as simple as 5 minutes on a cross trainer or a light jog around the oval or the backyard. The warm-ups in your twelve-week program are based around gym equipment. But you can replace these with any jogging or skipping exercise that gets your heart rate to 150 by the end.

Stretches should always be done at the end of a workout, which is when they work best (unless your physio or health practitioner recommends you do some muscle/joint-specific stretching before your workout).

equipment checklist

- good pair of training shoes — well-cushioned and with lateral support. It takes a week or two to break in new shoes, so have some bandaids around just in case. Make sure you do up your laces properly so your foot is not sliding around inside.
- for girls, a good sports bra
- workout towel
- water bottle
- heart-rate monitor
- dumbbells (light to medium)
- barbell (if you can)
- fitball
- skipping rope
- reliable alarm clock

These days, it is becoming more feasible to have exercise equipment in your home. For instance, my affordable One Active range has everything you need for a home fitness centre, including a treadmill, cross trainer and adjustable step. So even if you can't get to the local gym, you can do all the training you want!

the golden rules

The following rules apply to *every* exercise in this section. Don't forget to heed them, or you'll risk injury.

- **Breathe throughout the movement** — exhale on the power or pushing phase (the 'concentric' phase, where the muscle is contracting), and inhale on the return phase (the 'eccentric' phase, where the muscle is lengthening).
- **Ensure that your knees and feet track in the same direction** to avoid joint damage during knee bends.
- **Soften knees and elbows** by keeping them very slightly bent — never lock them straight.
- **Draw in your abdominals** and narrow your waist to support your back.
- **Lengthen your spine** by rolling your shoulders back and down and opening your chest.
- **Lengthen your neck** and avoid tensing it during exercise.
- **Pull your chin in slightly**, never letting your head roll backwards.

*'if you don't feel like a workout, do 10 minutes —
usually, once you start you'll want to keep going'*

toning exercises

I can't tell you how often I'm asked what exercises I do when I train. So, welcome to my office . . .

Weight training defines and reshapes your body, so I refer to it as toning. In each week of the twelve-week exercise program detailed in Chapter 10, I include two days of toning workouts, which use a combination of the exercises below. There are *stacks* of strength training exercises to choose from, so I've selected some of my favourites. Most require weights (dumbbells or barbells), but a few simply use body weight as the resistance. It would be best to join a gym for your weight training, but if you have the space at home, and are very organised and motivated, you *could* get by with an exercise mat, a fitball, a barbell and some dumbbells.

toning: lower body

For all the exercises in this section, remember the golden rules: chest elevated, shoulders rolled back and down, abs pulled in, neck long and chin in slightly. Once you become familiar with the exercises you can spice up your workout by challenging yourself with a little *variation*. Rhythm changes and bottom halves are great variations for squats, lunges and push-ups.

Rhythm changes: In squats, for example, instead of just squatting down and up at the same pace, try varying the rhythm by going down slowly to, say, the count of three, and then up quicker to a count of one. This is called a three/one. The variations are infinite — you can do a four/one, a two/two, a four/four, etc. So if, for example, you were doing three sets of squats, you can make the first one a two/two, the next one a three/one and the last one a four/four.

Bottom halves: This is where you repeat the bottom half of the movement (the hardest part) four or five times before you return to the top. For example, if you're doing your squats with a three/one rhythm, you go down slowly to the count of three, and when you're at the bottom, add five bottom halves. Oh my God! These *wreck*!

freestanding body-weight squat

1. Stand tall with your heels hip-width apart, your feet slightly angled out and your arms by your sides.

2. Imagine you are about to take a seat. Inhale as you bend your legs, and lower your hips until your thighs are almost parallel to the floor. At the same time extend your arms forward. At the bottom of the movement your knees should not be further forward than your toes and your chest should be proud.

3. Exhale as you push through your heels, squeeze your butt and return to the start position without locking out your knees.

'squats are my all-time favourite leg exercise — you'll get great legs, a tight butt and you'll blow off calories like crazy!'

barbell squat

1. Stand tall with your heels slightly wider than hip-width apart and your feet slightly angled out. Place the barbell on the fleshy part of your upper back and let the tension you feel between your shoulder blades help support the bar.

2. Inhale as you bend your legs and lower your hips until your thighs are almost parallel to the floor. Your knees should not be further forward than your toes. Keep your chest proud and your back long.

3. Exhale as you push through your heels and squeeze your butt to return to the start position. Use a mirror, if you can, to check that your knees stay in line with your toes.

80

fitball squat

1. Place a fitball between you and a wall so the ball is comfortably supporting your lower back. Step your feet forward and shoulder-width apart so that your heels are wider than your hips and your feet slightly angled out. Let your arms hang by your sides. If you're using dumbbells, grip them firmly.

2. Inhale as you bend your legs, and lower your hips until your thighs are almost parallel to the floor. At the bottom of the movement your knees should not be further forward than your toes. Because you're leaning against the ball your body will remain upright.

3. Exhale as you push through your heels and squeeze your butt to return to the start position.

VARIATIONS **Fitball squat with dumbbells:** this will make you work even harder.
Fitball squat with wide stance: this will recruit the muscles in your inner thighs more — just be sure that your knees go in the same direction as your feet, which should be pointing out slightly.

fitball hamstring curl

1. Lie on the floor with your arms beside you, palms facing down. Place your heels and calf muscles on the fitball. Have your feet about hip-width apart and flex your toes back towards you. Lift your hips up off the floor and lock your midsection tight so that your body is straight and is supported by your shoulders.

2. Keeping your torso strong, bend your knees and use your heels to roll the ball towards your butt. Keep your feet flexed and squeeze the backs of your legs and your inner thighs.

3. Roll the ball back to the start position, keeping your body taut.

'a great exercise for the backs of your legs, and your inner thighs too!'

'don't lean forward as you move down, and watch that front knee; make sure it doesn't drift forward past your toes'

static lunge

1. Stand tall, hands on hips, and take a long step **back** keeping your feet hip-width apart for balance. Keep your weight evenly distributed on both legs, your front knee slightly bent, and your weight on the ball of your back foot (the heel is up). Your feet will stay in this position for the whole exercise, so make sure you feel balanced.

2. Keeping the body tall, inhale as you bend your back knee towards the floor. Try to make a right angle with each leg — the front knee should remain above the ankle and not shoot forward past it. If this happens you need to lengthen your stride.

3. Inhale as you come up, pushing up through the front heel to engage your butt. Your movement should be up and down — *not* forwards and backwards.

Note: You are not 'stepping' with this exercise — your feet remain static.

VARIATIONS A **supported static lunge** is good for beginners – stand next to a bench, chair or fence at waist height, and use one hand to steady yourself as you drop into the lunge. A **static lunge with dumbbells or barbell** really ups the ante. But don't use these until you've practised stacks of lunges first.

forward power lunge

1. Stand tall, hands on hips, looking straight ahead.

2. Inhale and take a long step **forward**, keeping your feet hip-width apart and your weight evenly distributed between your front and back legs. *Both* legs should be bent at an angle of 90 degrees.

3. Exhale and powerfully push off your front foot to get you back to start position. Repeat for the opposite leg and then alternate legs, or do several reps on one side before you swap.

VARIATIONS Try a **forward power lunge with dumbbells**.
A **backward power lunge** will improve your technique.

'lunges will shred your legs like there's no tomorrow!'

dynamic lunge

1. Find a low, solid platform around 15–30 centimetres high (e.g. a step) and stand on it.

2. Take a long step back, keeping your feet hip-width apart and the heel of your back foot up. Both legs should be bent at 90 degrees.

3. Push off your back foot, tap the step with it and step back again. Repeat with the same leg several times then swap. To help with your balance, use your arms as if you are running.

VARIATION **Dynamic lunge with dumbbells:** the added weight will really test your balance, so slow down.

step-ups

1. Stand tall in front of a low bench or chair.

2. Step your right foot up onto the bench placing it flat.

3. Push up through the right leg and hips to place the left foot on the bench.

4. Now step back down with the right foot followed by the left. Repeat in the same order. Maintain the start position posture perfectly throughout.

VARIATIONS Wear a backpack with a medicine ball in it. Try **step-ups with dumbbells** or a **barbell**, but don't use weights first-up – they can be a bit scary if you trip.

'a much higher step for those ready to advance'

sumo squat with barbell

1. Stand with your heels widely spaced apart and your feet angled out. The wider stance means you will be using more muscles than a regular barbell squat. Place the barbell on the fleshy part of your upper back and let the tension you feel between your shoulder blades help support the bar.

2. Inhale as you bend your legs and lower your hips until your thighs are almost parallel to the floor. Keep your back strong.

3. Exhale as you push through your heels and return to the start position.

ACCESS TO A GYM? You could use the leg press machine instead.

84

toning: upper body — back

In all of the 'pulling' exercises, which we mostly perform when working the back muscles, the emphasis can be shifted simply by changing your grip on the bar. Traditionally, wide grips are most commonly prescribed by trainers, but you can also use a medium or narrow grip, or you can change your hand position from a palms-forward (overhand) to a palms-facing (underhand) grip. Is one hand position more effective than another? Not really — they all work the back muscles.

Put simply, overhand and underhand grips partially flex the lats from the start position. The best thing to do is to try them — do a set of each and you will feel the shift in emphasis and you'll also feel different muscles chipping in to help out (for example, an underhand grip will also recruit your biceps). Most importantly, all of these variations are 'compound', which means you're working lots of muscles at the same time — *exactly* what you want for maximum calorie-burning.

'always exhale on the exertion phase of a weight workout — don't hold your breath'

bent-over fly

1. Stand with your feet shoulder-width apart. Bend at the waist so that your torso is approximately 45 degrees to the floor. Hold the dumbbells straight down with your arms slightly bent.
2. Exhale as you raise your arms to the side until your hands are level with your shoulders. Keep your back strong.
3. Inhale and lower your arms back to the start position.

ACCESS TO A GYM? Do **lat pull-downs** with a wide grip (always bring the bar to the front of your body, never behind).

towel pulls

1. Take a sweat towel and loop it around a fixed pole or tree at chest height. Alternatively, get a friend to hold it. Grasp one end of the towel in each hand and place your feet near the base of the pole, shoulder-width apart. Lean back, letting the towel take your body weight.

2. Brace your abs, lift your chest and exhale as you pull yourself towards the pole, tucking your elbows in and squeezing your shoulder blades together.

3. Pause, inhale and control your return to the start position.

ACCESS TO A GYM? Do **assisted chins**. For beginners start with a weight that represents approximately 70 per cent of your body weight.

VARIATION Make it harder by putting on a heavy backpack.

dumbbell rows

1. Select a set of medium/heavy dumbbells and place one knee on a bench or chair. Support yourself by placing your free hand on the bench/chair and your other foot on the ground. Square up your shoulders and hips and lock yourself into a strong position with a long, straight back. Allow the dumbbells to hang directly below your shoulder.

2. Exhale as you pull the dumbbells up to your hip, keeping your elbow close to your torso and parallel to the floor.

3. Pause, and inhale as you lower the dumbbells back to the start position. (In the workouts section later, I'll always expect you to do fifteen repetitions with your left arm, followed by fifteen with your right.)

'think of this one as practice for starting your lawnmower — hold your core strong and avoid twisting through the shoulders and hips'

toning: upper body — chest

These six exercises are great for building upper body strength and are easy to do either at home or in the gym.

chest press with barbell

1. Lie on the floor (or on a bench) and, with arms outstretched and your hands slightly wider than shoulder-width apart, grip the barbell above your chest in line with your nipples. Your feet can be either on the bench or on the ground. (You may be more stable on the ground, but you'll need to be careful not to arch your back. Do whatever works best for you.)

2. Keep your midsection braced and inhale as you lower the barbell to about 10 cm above your chest.

3. Keep your chest elevated and exhale as you press the barbell back to the start position.

VARIATION A **chest press with barbell on an incline bench** will work different muscles.

'this is another exercise where it's easy to hurt your shoulders, so always keep the bar over your chest, never over your face'

chest press with dumbbells

1. Lie on a bench or on the ground (I'm on an incline bench in the picture) and, with straight arms, hold the dumbbells firmly above your shoulders around 10 cm apart. Your feet can either be on the bench or on the ground.

2. Keep your midsection braced and inhale as you lower the dumbbells towards the outside of your chest.

3. Keep the chest proud and abs pulled in as you exhale and press the dumbbells back to the top, finishing with them about 10 cm apart.

VARIATIONS This exercise is great whether you're on the **floor**, on a **flat bench** or on an **incline bench** at a gym.

'both arms work independently, so you may discover one side of your body is stronger than the other (very common); these exercises will help to correct it'

chest press with dumbbells on fitball

1. Sit on the edge of the fitball and rest some light/medium dumbbells on your thighs. Walking your feet forward, roll down the fitball and lower your shoulders so that your body is horizontal.

2. Lift the dumbbells above your head, holding them approximately 10 cm apart with straight arms.

3. Keep your midsection braced and inhale as you lower the dumbbells towards the outside of your chest.

4. Exhale as you press the dumbbells back to the top, keeping them 10 cm apart.

push-ups on knees

1. Kneel on the ground and walk your hands forward until they are slightly wider than shoulder-width apart. Straighten your arms, keep your torso long and strong and look directly ahead at the floor. Your knees can be hip-width apart or together.
2. Keeping your abs pulled in, inhale, bend your elbows and lower your upper body until your chest is about 10 cm off the floor.
3. Exhale as you straighten your arms to return to the start position.

'don't "shrug" those shoulders, and keep your bum down — at the bottom of the movement your hands and elbows should be aligned with your chest'

push-ups on toes

1. With your arms straight and slightly wider than shoulder-width apart, support your body on hands and toes. Your toes can be hip-width apart or together.
2. Inhale as you bend your arms and lower your upper body (keeping it strong and straight) until your chest is about 10 cm off the floor.
3. Exhale as you straighten the arms to return to the start position.

VARIATIONS Place your **hands on a bench**, and your knees or feet on the floor. Place your **feet on a bench**, and your hands on the floor.

'there's a good reason why not many people can do full-length push-ups — you have to be strong!'

walking push-ups with one hand elevated

This exercise can be performed either on your knees or on your toes (advanced).

1. Place one hand on the end of a low bench and the other hand on the floor. Your hands should be slightly wider than shoulder-width apart. Lengthen your torso, draw your abs in, expand your chest and drop your shoulders down away from your ears. Keep your neck long and your chin tucked in, and look at the floor directly ahead.

2. Bend your arms and inhale as you lower your upper body to about 10 cm off the floor.

3. Exhale as you straighten your arms to return to the start position, then hold your body strong as you swap hands to the other side and alternate the push-up.

VARIATIONS **Walking push-ups on floor** (i.e. without using a low bench).
Walking push-ups with medicine ball: place one hand on a medicine ball, perform one rep, then roll it across to your other hand and perform another one, and so on. Great stuff!

'the "walking" component really smashes core muscles; you can "walk" your body after each repetition or perform three to five reps on each side before swapping'

toning: arms and shoulders

Let's face it — everyone loves a good set of shoulders! The exercises in this section are my faves for upper body strength in the arms and shoulders.

standing shoulder press

1. Holding a barbell (or dumbbells) stand tall with your feet in a staggered stance. Your front knee should be soft and take most of your body weight; the ball of your back foot should be on the floor, your back leg acting as a prop to stop you from leaning backwards. You should feel rock solid.

2. Keeping your midsection braced, exhale as you drive the barbell towards the ceiling keeping it slightly forward of your face at the top of the movement. Do not lock out your elbows, keep them slightly bent, and do not push the bar back behind your head (or I will beat you and then give you my chiropractor's number).

3. Inhale as you carefully lower the barbell to the start position. Look forward throughout the movement and take care not to arch your back.

VARIATION **Standing shoulder press with dumbbells:** hold the dumbbells close to the shoulders, then exhale as you drive them towards the ceiling, aiming them to finish about 10 cm apart.

'concentrate on maintaining good posture to really get the most out of this exercise'

standing biceps curl with barbell

1. Holding the barbell in a natural carrying position, stand
   tall with one foot forward and one back. Your front knee
   should be soft and the ball of your back foot acting as a
   prop to stop you from leaning backwards.
2. Exhale as you raise the bar to your upper chest keeping
   your upper arms parallel with your body, and your elbows
   in. Avoid letting the bar collapse against your chest.
3. Keeping the midsection tight, inhale as you lower the
   bar to the start position. Your upper arms should remain
   still. Do not let your elbows point behind you on the way
   down or in front of you on the way up. The only direction
   they should be pointing is *down*. Keep your body still and
   avoid rocking or swaying.

'you should feel punished after curls —
I've had my heart rate at 163 with this exercise!'

triceps bench dips

1. Sit on a low bench and grip the edge.
   Support your weight through your arms
   and shoulders and walk your legs forward
   so that your thighs are parallel to the floor
   and your feet flat.
2. Inhale as you lower your body until your
   upper arms are almost horizontal.
3. Exhale as you drive yourself up to the start
   position, contracting the muscles in the
   back of your arms.

VARIATIONS Put your feet on another bench.
Increase the resistance further by placing a
medicine ball or weight plate on your lap.

'the most common mistake
here is slouching and
letting your shoulders roll
over — keep your chest up!'

toning: core

The main focus with all abdominal training is to pull or draw your abs inwards throughout the entire movement, both up and down. Think of 'narrowing' the waist rather than 'thickening' it.

crunch

1. Lie on the floor and bend your knees so that your feet are flat on the floor. Draw in your abs, narrowing your waist, and place your hands palms down beside you, across your chest or — the hardest option — behind your head. (If your hands are behind your head, keep your elbows out of sight and avoid pulling on your head and bending your neck.)
2. Keeping your abs tight, exhale as you roll or 'crunch' your upper torso. Keep your chin in and look forward.
3. Keep your abs drawn in and inhale as you lower yourself back down to the start position.

VARIATION **Crunch with medicine ball:** holding a medicine ball increases the intensity.

supported crunch with medicine ball

1. Sit on the floor and tuck your feet under a support such as a weighted bar, ledge or even the edge of your couch. Bend your knees to 90 degrees and roll back, lying flat and holding the medicine ball directly above your chest.
2. Exhale as you lift your body upwards towards the ceiling.
3. Drawing your abs in tight, inhale and lower yourself down to the start position.

VARIATIONS **Supported crunch without medicine ball:** using the medicine ball really challenges, so start off without it if it's too much. **Supported crunch with twist:** lift one shoulder to the opposite knee for several repetitions or alternate.

fitball crunch with twist

1. Sit on the fitball and roll yourself down until it's under your lower back, and your thighs and torso are parallel with the floor. Draw your abs inwards, narrowing your waist, and place your hands either across your chest or behind your head.

2. Exhale as you raise your body up to an angle of around 45 degrees, adding a twist by lifting one shoulder towards the opposite leg.

3. Keeping your abs pulled in, inhale and lower yourself back down to the start position.

VARIATIONS **Fitball crunch with medicine ball:** try it without the twist first, then try lifting the opposite leg off the floor during the twist to really test your balance.

'try to aim your knees at the roof rather than bringing them to your chest when you crunch — keep your chin in and your head on the floor'

reverse crunch

1. Lie on your back and bend your knees, inhaling as you lift your legs so that your thighs are at 90 degrees and directly over your hips. Draw your abdominals down to hollow out the belly and keep your lower back firm against the floor. Place your arms beside you, palms down.

2. Exhale as you lift the lower half of your body towards the ceiling.

3. Inhale as you lower carefully to your start position.

NOTE: Stay away from 'swinging' the legs. Rather, it's a small and intense squeeze and lift.

double crunch

1. Lie on your back and lift your legs above you keeping your knees bent at 90 degrees and directly over your hips. Hollow out your belly so that your lower back is firm against the floor and place your hands behind your head.

2. Exhale as you lift the upper and lower half of your body at the same time. Think of squeezing yourself into a tiny ball. Keep your elbows out and avoid pulling on your head.

3. Inhale as you uncurl back to the start position, going slowly to protect your back.

NOTE: there's no photo for this but just add the **crunch** (p.93) and **reverse crunch** (p.94) together and you've got it!

'what can I say? ouch! these work!'

leg extensions

1. Lie on your back and lift your legs above you keeping your knees bent at 90 degrees and directly over your hips. Place your arms beside you, palms down, and keep your lower back firm against the floor.

2. Keeping one leg in place, exhale and straighten the other leg away from you until you can no longer keep your abs drawn in. As soon as you feel your abs 'pop' outwards, or your lower back start to arch away from the floor, you have extended the leg too far. Pull your leg back until you can reset your abs inwards. The stronger you get, the further you will be able to extend your leg. Keep your head on the floor.

leg extensions with twisting crunch

1. Lie on your back and lift your legs above you keeping your knees bent at 90 degrees and directly over your hips. Place your hands behind your head for support (avoid pulling and bending your neck) and keep your elbows wide and out of sight.

2. Exhale and extend one leg as you simultaneously lift the shoulder on the same side towards the bent knee. You must keep your abs pulled in throughout the entire movement. As soon as you feel your abs 'pop' out you have extended the leg too far, so pull your leg back to reset your abs.

lower body twist

1. Lie on your back and lift your knees over your hips. Place your arms outstretched beside you, palms down.
2. 'Glue' your legs and feet together. Inhale as you slowly lower both legs to one side, to about halfway down, keeping your shoulders on the floor.
3. Exhale as you slowly drag the legs back to centre.
4. Repeat on the other side.

VARIATION Increase the resistance by lowering the legs further, or by extending the legs at an angle greater than 90 degrees.

'try to keep the upper half of your body relaxed and in perfect posture, and really wring out that waistline!'

side plank

1. Lie on your side, raise youself up on one elbow, palm flat, and 'stack' your shoulders, hips, knees and feet perpendicular to the floor. Inhale as you open up your chest, stabilising yourself on your elbow and hip. Work from your knees to start with, bending them at 90 degrees.
2. Exhale as you lift your hip so your body is in a straight line from your knees to your head. Imagine you are pushing up 'out' of your shoulder, which will enable you to draw the shoulders back and down and lengthen your neck.
3. Extend your other arm straight up to the roof to help you open up your chest. If you're working from your feet, keep your legs long and strong. Breathe and hold for thirty seconds to a minute.

'the bottom one is harder'

96

hover on knees or toes

1. Lie facedown on the floor. Place your hands forward and flat, elbows directly under your shoulders. Lengthen your neck, pull your chin in, and look at your hands. Keep your knees on the floor and hip-width apart. Your body should be like a plank of wood, so keep your abs pulled in.

2. Get the feeling of pushing yourself away from the floor to stabilise your shoulders. Keep breathing steadily and easily, and keep your body in alignment. Tuck your tailbone under very slightly.

3. When you're ready to try your toes, start on your toes and stay for as long as you can before finishing the time on your knees. Work up to a minute.

'try not to roll forward or backward through the shoulders or hips; instead stay nice and square — you will feel the underside of your body really firing up'

toning: prone work

I find most of my de-conditioned clients really need this type of exercise, and it's often due to so many of us spending a lot of time behind a desk, behind a wheel or on our feet, which is when we tend to be lax through the upper and lower back and through the core. They can be done anywhere and you don't really need any equipment.

kneeling core and balance

1. Start on all fours with your hands directly under your shoulders and your knees directly under your hips. Draw your waistline in, pulling your bellybutton up.

2. Maintaining your balance, slowly reach out with your right arm long and strong as you push through the heel to extend your left leg in the opposite direction no higher than the line of the torso. You should feel like you are stretching both ways. Try to minimise 'wobbling' by scooping up your abs and making your belly hollow.

3. Continue to move your limbs in and out slowly, really 'wringing out' your muscles. Do several repetitions on one side before swapping. (In some workouts I get you to hold the last rep for a minute.)

VARIATION: You can change the training effect by extending the opposite limbs out on a diagonal. This really fires up those core muscles!

'most people are really wobbly to start with, but once you get tuned in to your body you will start to become strong and still'

alternating back extension

1. Lie on your stomach with your arms straight out in front and your legs extended behind you.

2. Exhale and slowly lift your right arm, your left leg and your chest off the floor simultaneously. You *must* keep looking straight down at the floor with your chin pulled in and your neck relaxed (otherwise you'll hurt your neck).

3. Inhale and lower, then repeat on the opposite side.

'keep your toes flexed to avoid cramping in your calf'

'a lot of people seem to stick their chin out and then wonder why their necks are getting sore — tuck your chin in and lengthen your neck'

fitball alternating back extension

1. Drape yourself over a fitball on your stomach with both arms and legs extended so your toes just touch the floor to keep you balanced.

2. Exhale and slowly lift your right arm and your left leg. Remember — keep looking straight down with your chin tucked in and neck soft.

3. Inhale and lower, then swap sides.

VARIATION Do several reps on one side before you swap.

'go slowly and really feel the squeeze through the back, butt and back of the leg'

aeroplanes

1. Lie on your stomach with both arms outstretched at right angles, forehead on the floor and legs shoulder-width apart.

2. Keeping your toes on the floor, exhale and slowly lift your upper body off the floor. You *must* keep looking straight down with your chin pulled in to avoid hurting your neck.

3. Tilt your body to one side as if you're a plane tipping its wing (keeping your neck aligned with your spine), reset to centre, inhale and lower your chest to the floor. Repeat for the opposite side.

supported back extension on fitball

1. Drape yourself over a fitball on your stomach and firmly grip a medicine ball between your ankles on the floor behind you. Place your hands either out in front of you or behind your head.

2. Exhale and slowly lift your upper body. Remember — keep looking straight down with your chin tucked in and neck soft.

3. Inhale and lower, then repeat.

'tuck that chin in and lengthen your neck, or you'll regret it when you wake up the next morning and you can't turn your head to turn the alarm clock off!'

fitness training

Cardiovascular fitness training is any kind of exercise that gets the heart rate up. Most trainers associate it with aerobic activity (running, cycling, etc.), but if you use my methods in the weight room (i.e. lots of super sets with not much rest in between), then you can be sure of getting a good cardiovascular response *whenever* you train. And when your heart is pumping and you're huffing and puffing, you're burning fat — and that's why we're here! Plus, you're getting fitter, which is why I call cardio workout days your *fitness* days in the workouts in Chapter 10.

We've covered plenty of exercises with weights, so now we'll go through a few calorie-smashers you can do either outside or inside. There are hundreds of cardiovascular exercises and drills to choose from, but these are the ones that I like to use because *I know they work!*

running

As we discovered in Chapter 7, walking is a waste of time for weight loss unless you either start negotiating some serious hills or you pump up the speed to around 6 to 8 kilometres per hour, which should have you puffing so hard that you can only say two or three words between breaths. Walking is really only a precursor to the *real* calorie burners — jogging and running.

If you think you're too big to run, let me tell you, I've worked with people well over 150 kilos and got them running within a few short weeks! So start injecting jogging into the mix. Come on! You *can* do it! Work up to, say, a 1-minute jog followed by a 2-minute walk and so on until you can jog your entire course without stopping.

But this process has *got* to work like a ratchet. You can *never* go backwards. From there improve your jogging time, and then increase the distance so that you are exercising for the same amount of time but jogging *all* the way. Now you are really chewing calories and getting fitter!

However, if you absolutely *cannot* jog or run due to a pre-existing injury, but you can walk, then I have the answer: get on the treadmill. First, walk as briskly as you can at, say, 5 km/h and then turn that sucker up to an incline of 15 per cent. Now your cardiovascular system is working at pretty much the same level as a jog, but with virtually no impact.

In Chapter 10, you'll see that you can use jogging as your warm-up, or as your 'final blast' at the end of a workout. If you are unable to get to the gym, or if someone is using your exercise space, get your trainers on and GO. Just make sure you go hard.

The difference between jogging and running is simply the speed at which you're travelling. Around 8 km/h is a jog, and anything over 10–11 km/h is a run, but it's all relative. What I consider jogging is running for a lot of my clients, but when I 'jog' with my mate Shannan, it's all I can do to keep up with him — it feels like sprinting to me!

Moving from brisk power walking to jogging and then up to running takes time, but it's all doable. Jogging on grass is more cushioning on joints; jogging on sand even more so and it's also good for strengthening the ankles, but it's a little tougher. Jogging or running outside is *very* different to jogging or running on a treadmill and I encourage my clients to do both. Treadmills are great, though, when it's pouring outside, and are safer for people who live in poorly lit areas but can only train at night.

Setting your route: Set out a route that you feel is achievable. It might be one block around your house or it might be two laps of the oval — it doesn't matter. First, take a drive around your neighbourhood and watch your odometer to work out how many kilometres it is to the park and back or around the block, etc. That way when you get out on the road, you'll know exactly how far you're running in each session — 1 kilometre might be longer than you think!

Set up the course, wear your watch and then go. Some days your focus will be about doing it in your best time; other days you will be happy with just getting the job done. Occasionally you will try to extend the course by adding another lap or two and who cares about the time? Mix it up.

Running technique: Watch your technique: remember to keep your abs pulled in, chest lifted, shoulders back and down, neck long, chin in, face relaxed. Try to land softly without thumping your feet. The heel should strike the ground first and then naturally roll onto the ball of the foot. Use your legs like shock absorbers and try to keep your knees aligned with your toes, rather than having them roll or cave in. Think light. Swing your arms and get yourself into a steady rhythm.

Most of all, just stay calm and relaxed, don't listen to the negative self-talk telling you to stop, or that you are dying. You don't have to beat any world record, you just have to have a go. My experience tells me that you *will* surprise yourself!

The following variations are great little running drills that you can introduce into your training that will help you improve your running technique and fitness.

treadmills

One person I worked with had only ever done her running training on the treadmill so her first outdoor run was a rude shock. This was because when she ran on her treadmill at 0 per cent gradient, it was the equivalent of running *downhill*. All she was doing was running to stop herself from falling over – not propelling herself forward. (To simulate running outdoors, always set the gradient on your treadmill at a minimum of 2 per cent.)

She was able to get fitter faster by adding some outdoor training to her schedule, and it also gave some freshness to her training.

stair runs

Find a big flight of stairs (the more the better! At least twenty!) and run up it, then walk down. Take one step at a time at first, then graduate to taking two steps at a time. You may need to hang onto the handrail until you get your confidence. Stair runs can also double as a fitness test. How long does it take you to get to the top? Try to beat your time, though always use the same flight of stairs.

hill runs

These can be done either outside or on a treadmill. Run up a hill (sand hills are fantastic if you live near any), walk back down it and repeat. If you're using a treadmill, remember to rest your feet on the side boards as you increase the treadmill's gradient and speed. Then lower yourself onto the belt and run on a steep incline for 1 minute before jumping your feet out to the side boards and reducing the incline and the speed back down to a walk for a minute. Some treadmills can be programmed to do this – ask your gym staff to show you how.

'going for a run is a great mood-booster!'

treadmill interval sprints

These can be done either outside or on a treadmill. When you're outside, sprint a specific distance, e.g. the length of a football field, then walk back. Time yourself then try to beat your time.

If you're using a treadmill, rest your feet on the side boards as you increase the treadmill's speed up to your sprint speed. Supporting your weight on the side handles, lift and lower yourself onto the belt, sprint for 30 seconds and then jump out to the side. (Note: this is an advanced drill, so practise jumping on and off at a lower speed first!)

fast low-step running

Find a low step or take an aerobics step, stand in front of it and quickly step up onto it and back down — right left up, right left down, right left up, right left down — as fast as you can for a set time or a set number of reps. Work the arms to give you more speed.

skipping

Skipping is a great way to get your heart rate up, work on your coordination and help with your fitness. There's a good reason why boxers do it! Get yourself a skipping rope and start a competition at home. Who can do the most skips nonstop? Keep a record, stick it up on the fridge to inspire the family, and make sure someone always witnesses any attempt. You don't want any fouls called!

'try everything once — you'll probably find lots of different exercises that you enjoy'

cycling

Cycling offers a great cardiovascular workout, but without the joint impact. For those who are very overweight or injured, cycling is a fantastic option. It is often prescribed for those who are rehabilitating from knee and hip injury or surgery.

I totally rate indoor classes as you can't get hit by a car and you can't fall off! Indoor bikes can do just about everything you can do outside. In fact, many professional cyclists use them for their training.

rowing machine

Rowing rocks! I advise you to get one of the gym staff to show you how to use the rower, and then just practise. I use this equipment as a great warm-up exercise and also as a fantastic cardio burst with 500-metre sprints. Any time under 3 minutes for a 500-metre sprint is good. Under 2 minutes is *amazing*.

agility training

Being agile enables you to rapidly change direction without losing speed, balance or control and comprises lots of short, sharp movements. The best thing about this type of training is that you don't need *any* equipment except a good pair of trainers!

sideways running

Starting with your right foot, run three to five steps sideways to the right. On the last step your right foot should 'stick' as you first drop your weight into that leg before pushing off with it and stepping out with your left. (When you plant your foot on the last step your whole foot should be in contact with the ground and slightly angled out in the direction you were heading. Make sure your knee is pointing in the same direction as your toes. Keep your shoulders back and down, chest up, abs in and swing your arms to give you momentum.) The timing should feel like 'one, two, drop and push, one, two, drop and push'.

forward and backward jumps

With your feet hip-width apart, point your toes straight ahead, keep your knees soft like shock absorbers, pull your abs in and elevate your chest. Jump over a line (or a rope or towel) and back again. Land softly!

ice skaters on the spot

Lay a towel down or set up a low-step platform and take a long low leap over it sideways. Swing your arms strongly in the direction you are travelling and land the foot solidly with the toes and knee aligned (slightly angled out). Bend into the leg before you push off, leading with the other leg and repeating for the opposite side.

'vary your exercise routine — it should be fun, not a chore'

ski jumps

Keeping your toes and knees aligned and your knees soft, switch on your abs, lift your chest and jump sideways over a line, towel or rope on the ground. Pump your arms to maintain your momentum.

jumping jacks

Start with your feet together, then jump them about shoulder-width apart. Try to land softly and have your heels contact the ground. Toes are slightly turned out as are the knees (a lot of people seem to 'cave in' their knees — ouch!), and let your legs act like shock absorbers as you jump your feet back together. Swing your arms out to the side or overhead. Keep your abs in, chest up, shoulders back.

'keep pushing yourself — try to jump higher or bend lower each time'

basketball jumps

These are similar to jumping jacks, but work from side to side. Take a low long step to the right, bend through the legs, keep your knees aligned with your toes. Step the left foot in and spring off from both feet to shoot your basket then repeat on the other side. Swing your arms out wide in the step then scoop them through for the shot. The lower you go the higher you jump.

over-the-fence jumps

Take a bench and standing on one side bend down and grip the edges on either side. Using both feet spring yourself up and over to the other side and then spring straight back again. Do not stop or double bounce and try to keep your feet together. You'll need to keep your shoulders braced to support your weight and your midsection switched on.

*'just think of yourself as an exerciser;
it's now a part of who you are'*

boxing

When I first hooked up with a boxing coach, Oh. My. God! He worked me so hard I thought I was going to bring up a lung or a kidney or both! I blew up 836 calories in 50 minutes!

It's hard to do boxing on your own if you've never really done it before, and although many health clubs have equipment you can use, it's always a good idea to get some proper advice. My suggestions:

- Go to a boxing class at your health club and just join in (maybe take a friend if you are a bit nervous, that way you can partner up)

- Get a personal trainer who specialises in boxing. They should be able to show you how to punch the bag so that you can go at it when you're on your own.

flexibility training

In my experience, no one ever stretches enough. Stretching always seems to get thrown in at the end of a session as a token gesture — I am guilty of this myself. Stretching helps prevent injuries, and is best done after a workout when you are nice and warm. Having said that, it's important to remember that this is *not* a stretching manual, it's a weight-loss manual. I also know that at this stage of the book most people will flick through a few pretty photos of stretches and say 'Yeah, whatever . . .' and ignore the stretches themselves.

To avoid that happening, and to give you the best chance of incorporating stretching into your routine, I've put together a basic sequence that loosens up all the big muscle groups.

It's not a glossary of stretches — it's a sequence that starts with the large muscles and finishes with the small ones. Learn the sequence and incorporate it into the end of every training session. Once you have learned the stretches and understand the pattern you should be able to run through them in about 5 to 10 minutes.

It's definitely not the *only* way to stretch, it's just a guide to get you loosened up after your workout and in the hustle-and-bustle world in which we live, I reckon if I can get you doing this much I'll be happy. The key here is to make sure you get to a yoga, stretch or BodyBalance class occasionally to help loosen off your newly developed muscles — and to show off your fabulous new body!

basic stretching sequence

In the sequence below, try to hold each stretch for approximately one minute. Keep breathing, and try to sink deeper into the stretch as you exhale. Do not bounce into your stretches or hold your breath.

back twist

Straighten your legs and lengthen out your body. Bring one leg up into a right angle and using the opposite hand gently pull your knee across your body, gently twisting your lower back. Extend the other arm out, trying to keep both shoulders on the ground. Turn your head away from the bent knee. Keep breathing, and with every exhalation gently sink deeper into the stretch. Repeat on the opposite side.

lower back stretch

Lying on the ground, roll your knees up into your chest, wrap your arms around your legs and gently pull them in. If you can't reach around your legs, wrap a towel across your shins to pull them in.

hip opener

Bring one leg up into a right angle and leaving your foot on the floor, cross the other leg over it. Use your hand to gently press the crossed knee away to open the hip. To get more out of the stretch, reach through and clasp your hands behind your leg, and gently pull both legs towards you (pictured). If you can't reach, use a towel. If it's quite easy to reach, and you want to increase the stretch, lace your hands in front of your shin. Repeat on the opposite side.

hamstring stretch

Keeping one leg bent with the foot flat on the ground, bring the other leg towards you. Clasp your hands behind your knee (or calf if you can) and lift your leg and point it to the ceiling. Keep it slightly bent and flex your foot, and you will feel the stretch in your hamstring. Again, if you need to, wrap a towel around your calf or shoe to gently pull your leg towards you. Increase the stretch effect by straightening the base leg out. Repeat on the opposite side.

child's pose

With your knees shoulder-width apart, slide your buttocks back onto your heels and extend your arms in front, lowering your forehead towards the ground. In yoga this is known as the 'pose of the child' (not judging by the screaming kids I see!)

'stretching helps both performance and recovery'

inner thigh stretch

1. These are particularly good if you are doing a lot of running. Kneel on all fours and, keeping your arms straight, extend your leg out to the side with your foot pointing forwards.

2. Uncurl the toes on your supporting leg and slowly sit your butt down, dropping onto your elbows at the same time. Feel the stretch running down the inside of your straight-leg thigh.

3. Return to all fours, straightening your arms and stepping the leg back before repeating on the other side.

quadriceps stretch

Stand tall and, extending one arm for balance, curl your leg up behind you and grab your foot with the same hand. Keeping your knees together, gently pull your heel into your butt. Draw your abs in and pull your shoulders back and down, elevating your chest. Think about tucking your tailbone under to get more of a stretch. If your balance is good, take both hands behind you and hold your foot, and fully expand your chest and pull your shoulders back. Repeat on the opposite leg.

calf stretch

Push against a solid wall or railing and step one foot back. Keep the toes of the back foot pointing straight ahead and push the heel into the ground. Now lean into the wall to feel the stretch in the upper calf. Bend the back knee to deepen the stretch.

chest stretch

Stand tall, draw your abs in, drop your shoulders and reach behind you, interlocking your fingers. Exhale into the stretch, keeping the chest lifted and shoulders down.

shoulder stretch

Take one arm across the body at shoulder height and hold it in place using the crook of your other elbow. Gently pull the straight arm towards you. Watch that your shoulder doesn't creep up — try to keep it down — and keep your neck long. Repeat on the opposite side.

triceps stretch

Bend one arm and take it behind your head. Using the other arm, hold the elbow and gently assist the stretch down. Keep the chest lifted and repeat on the opposite side.

neck stretch

Lift your chest and drop your shoulders down away from your ears. Very gently lower your head to one side (ear to shoulder). Repeat on the opposite side.

10 workout program

'if you miss a day, do not panic! get back on the horse, consistency is the key!'

NOW IT'S TIME TO COMBINE THE EXERCISES you learned in the previous chapter to build a workout program that will deliver a killer result. You'll probably find yourself referring back to the exercises frequently for the first week or so, but after that they'll become second nature.

For dramatic results, you must follow these workouts (along with the nutrition plan in 'Get Cooking'). It may seem daunting at first, especially if regular exercise is a whole new experience for you, but *I know you can do it!* I've trained hundreds of clients using these exercises *and they work!* Having said that, I want

you to be flexible. If you can't get to the gym, or someone's taken over the spare room, then jog, run, skip or cycle instead — as long as you're huffing and puffing, you're burning calories.

Each week will feature three days of fitness (cardio) training and two days of toning (weight) training and one day of core strength. On your fitness day you can either do the circuit I've designed, or choose one of the professional fitness classes I suggest. Most of the circuits will take you about fifty minutes, depending on how organised and focused you are. Most classes run for fifty minutes.

'make a plan — then go out and smash it!'

114

rough guide to dumbbell weights (kg)

| | female | | male | |
	upper body	lower body	upper body	lower body
light	1–5	5–7	6–10	10–15
medium	6–10	8–10	11–20	16–20
heavy	11–20	11–20	20+	20+

fitness days

- A fitness **circuit** is a series of exercises (**twenty** repetitions each) performed one after the other without any rests in between. In my workouts you must go *twice* **through** the whole circuit. Closer to the end of the twelve weeks you'll do the circuit *three* times.
- You can set up the circuits either in the gym, the group fitness room or even outside, as most of them use minimal equipment. However, you must check out your training schedule *before* your allotted exercise time, so you know exactly what you'll be doing and what you'll need.
- I've made Saturday a cardio training day, as most of my clients choose this day for their 'treat meal'. This way you can smash up the calories before you indulge.

toning days

- On toning days you can either choose a class like BodyPump, or do the weights program I've devised for you.

- Where possible, you need to do your weights in '**super sets**'. This is where you do two different exercises, one for the upper body and one for the lower(**fifteen repetitions each**), and repeat the pair two or three times through. This will keep your heart rate up and in doing so trash the calories. Super sets can be tricky if your gym is busy, however, so be flexible — if it's not possible to use two pieces of equipment at once, simply stay with one exercise for fifteen reps, have 45 seconds' rest and then go again for another fifteen reps before moving on to the next exercise.
- For the first two weeks the weights should be light: 1–5 kilograms for your upper body and 5–7 kilograms for your lower body, depending on your gender and the exercise (see the table above). **You must, however, increase your weights every two to three weeks to get the best results.** How much you increase your weights will depend on the exercise and your fitness, but you should be really heaving by the last rep.

warm-ups

- There is also a warm-up for every training session. You *must* try to get your heart rate up to 140–150 BPM by the end.
- If you're not using a gym, simply replace any treadmill, cross trainer or rowing machine warm-up with jogging or running (see pages 101–3 for running tips). Any 'final blasts' that use the same equipment can be substituted with a lap around the block or park — whatever gets your heart rate up.

stretch

Do the stretch sequence on pages 110–13 at the end of every workout. Note, however, that if you do a BodyBalance, Pilates, yoga or core class on your Friday workout you won't need to do the stretch sequence that day.

If you miss a day, *do not panic*! Get back on the horse. Don't beat yourself up and use it as an excuse to throw in the towel. Consistency is the key! Good luck and train *hard*!

michelle's seven-day workout diary

When you read this diary, you need to remember that I am a *professional* trainer, and that keeping fit is part of my job, so I have a pretty intense exercise routine. Plus I have to appear on national TV in lycra! But it doesn't give you the excuse to say, 'Oh, it's okay for her!' It's still hard for me and requires commitment and sweat, so you've got to get out there and do your bit. I usually break up my training into morning and afternoon sessions, though that also depends on my work commitments.

monday	am	run 10 kilometres (52 minutes)	596 calories
	pm	bodypump class (45 minutes)	410 calories
tuesday	am	basic training circuit (50 minutes)	580 calories
	pm	treadmill 10 km/h (15 minutes)	148 calories
wednesday	am	run 12 kilometres (60 minutes)	712 calories
	pm	weights session (30 minutes)	278 calories
thursday	am	boxing session (50 minutes)	758 calories
	pm	indoor cycle class (45 minutes)	468 calories
friday	am	run 12 kilometres (62 minutes)	736 calories
saturday	am	bodypump class (45 minutes)	419 calories
	am	bodyattack class (45 minutes)	502 calories
sunday		rest	

This week is about getting your body used to exercise and equipment. On your fitness days, if you choose the circuit, remember to do each exercise 20 times, and the whole set twice. On your toning days, you'll do 15 repetitions of each exercise in the 'super set' pair, but you must do each pair twice through

monday: fitness

WARM-UP Treadmill 5 mins (5 km/h, level 2)	**CLASS** (indoor cycle, step) or **CIRCUIT** ↓		STRETCH
	• Fast low-step running right leg (p. 104) • Fast low-step running left leg (p. 104) • Push-ups on knees (p. 89) • Freestanding body-weight squat (p. 80) • Standing shoulder press with light barbell or dumbbells (p. 91) • Static lunge with support (20 each leg) (p. 82) • Standing biceps curl with light barbell (p. 92)	**ABS** • Crunch (p. 93) • Crunch with right twist (p. 94) • Crunch with left twist (p. 94)	

tuesday: toning

WARM-UP Cross trainer 5 mins	**CLASS** (BodyPump) or **WEIGHTS** ↓		STRETCH
	• Bent-over fly (p. 85) + Sumo squat with barbells (p. 84) • Chest press with barbell (p. 87) + Fitball squat (p. 81) • Towel pulls (p. 86) + Static lunge with support (alternating legs) (p. 82) **FINAL BLAST** Treadmill 5 mins (5.5 km/h, incline level 2)	**ABS** • Crunch (p. 93) • Crunch with twist (p. 94) alternating left and right • Hover on knees (p. 97) 30 secs	

wednesday: fitness

WARM-UP Treadmill 5 mins (5 km/h, level 2)	**CLASS** (Boxing, indoor cycle, step) or **CIRCUIT** ↓		STRETCH
	• Ski jumps (p. 107) • Push-ups on knees (p. 89) • Standing biceps curl with barbell (p. 92) • Fast low-step running, right leg (p. 104) • Fast low-step running, left leg (p. 104) • Sprints (4 × 15m) • Standing shoulder press with dumbbells (p. 91) **FINAL BLAST** Treadmill 5 mins (5.5 km/h, level 2)	**ABS** • Reverse crunch (p. 94) • Leg extensions (p. 95) • Lower body twist (p. 96)	

'on your toning days, remember to do each pair of exercises ('super set') <u>twice through</u> before moving on to the next pair'

before moving on to the next pair. Try to spike your heart rate above 140 BPM several times during your workouts. Perform 20 repetitions of the abs exercises twice through (two 'sets') on all days.

Remember — do all circuits with URGENCY!

thursday: toning

WARM-UP Rowing machine 5 mins	CLASS (BodyPump) or **WEIGHTS** ↓		STRETCH
	• Chest press with dumbbells (p. 88) + Sumo squat with barbells (p. 84) • Bent-over fly (p. 85) + Step-ups with dumbbells (p. 84) • Standing shoulder press with barbell (p. 91) + Fitball hamstring curl (p. 81) **FINAL BLAST** Cross trainer 5 mins	**ABS** • Fitball crunch (p. 94) • Fitball crunch with right twist (p. 94) • Fitball crunch with left twist (p. 94)	

friday: light fitness, core strength and stretch

WARM-UP Cycle 15 mins (aim for 150+ heart rate by end)	CLASS (Pilates, yoga, BodyBalance, core) or **CIRCUIT** ↓	STRETCH (Hold each for 2 mins — omit if you do a class)
	• Kneeling core and balance (right arm and left leg, holding last for 1 minute) (p. 98) • Kneeling core and balance (left arm and right leg, holding last for 1 minute) (p. 98) • Alternating back extension (p. 99) • Crunch with left twist (p. 93) • Crunch with right twist (p. 93) • Lower body twist (p. 96) • Leg extensions (p. 95) • Reverse crunch (p. 94)	

saturday: fitness

WARM-UP Treadmill 10 mins (5 km/h, level 2)	CLASS (Hi-energy, indoor cycle, BodyAttack, step) or **CIRCUIT** ↓		STRETCH
	• Skipping (1 min) (p. 105) • Backward power lunge (alternating legs) (p. 83) • Ski jumps (p. 107) • Standing biceps curl with barbell (p. 92) • Basketball jumps (p. 108) • Standing shoulder press with light dumbbells (p. 91) **FINAL BLAST** Treadmill 5 mins (5.5 km/h, level 2)	**ABS** • Crunch with right twist (p. 93) • Crunch with left twist (p. 93) • Lower body twist (p. 96)	

'ski jumps and basketball jumps can be tough when you're just starting out, so start small and build up'

Now you're getting it! Remember that if you're not doing classes, you need to do 20 reps of each exercise in the fitness circuits, 15 of each in the weights workouts and 20 of the abs exercises, all sets twice through. Try to spike your heart rate above 140 BPM several times during your workouts.

monday: fitness

WARM-UP Treadmill 5 mins (5 km/h, level 2)	**CLASS** (Boxing, indoor cycle, step) *or* **CIRCUIT** ↓		STRETCH
	• Skipping (1 minute) (p. 105) • Push-up on knees (p. 84) • Basketball jumps (p. 108) • Triceps bench dips (p. 92) • Backward power lunge (20 each leg) (p. 83) • Standing shoulder press with dumbbells (p. 91) • Sprints (4 × 15m) **FINAL BLAST** Treadmill 5 mins (5.5 km/h, level 2)	**ABS** • Hover on knees (30 secs) (p. 97) • Fitball crunch (p. 94) • Fitball crunch with twist (p. 94)	

tuesday: toning

WARM-UP Cross trainer 5 mins (5 km/h, level 2)	**CLASS** (BodyPump) *or* **WEIGHTS** ↓		STRETCH
	• Towel pulls (p. 86) + Barbell squat (p. 80) • Push-ups on toes to maximum, then finish on knees (p. 89) + Backward power lunge (alternating legs) with light dumbbells (p. 83) • Dumbbell rows (p. 86) 15 each arm + Fitball squat with dumbbells (p. 81) **FINAL BLAST** Treadmill 5 mins (5.5 km/h, level 2)	**ABS** • Lower body twist (p. 96) • Leg extensions (p. 95) • Crunch (p. 93)	

wednesday: fitness

WARM-UP Skipping 3 mins, cycle 3 mins (aim for 150+ heart rate by end)	**CLASS** (Boxing, indoor cycle, step) *or* **CIRCUIT** ↓		STRETCH
	• Sprints (4 × 15m) • Standing biceps curl with barbell (p. 92) • Ice skaters on the spot (p. 107) • Triceps bench dips (p. 92) • Sprints (4 × 15m) • Forward power lunge (alternating legs) (p. 83) • Ski jumps (p. 107) **FINAL BLAST** Treadmill 5 mins (5.5 km/h, level 2)	**ABS** • Leg extensions with twisting crunch (p. 95) • Reverse crunch (p. 94) • Crunch with twist (p. 93) alternating right and left	

'push-ups on toes are hard, but brilliant for core strength — try just doing three or four, and even if they aren't very deep, it's a start!'

thursday: toning

WARM-UP Cross trainer 5 mins (using the handles)	CLASS (Body Pump) or **WEIGHTS** ↓		STRETCH
	• Bent-over fly (p. 85) + Sumo squat with barbell (p. 84) • Chest press with dumbbells (p. 88) + Static lunge with dumbbells (15 each leg) (p. 82) • Standing shoulder press with dumbbells (p. 91) + Fitball hamstring curl (p. 81) **FINAL BLAST** Treadmill 5 min (5.5 km/h, level 2)	**ABS** • Supported crunch (p. 93) • Supported crunch with medicine ball (p. 93) • Supported crunch with twist (p. 93)	

friday: light fitness, core strength and stretch

WARM-UP Cycle 15 mins or treadmill 15 mins (5.5 km/h, level 2)	CLASS (Pilates, yoga, BodyBalance, core) or **CIRCUIT** ↓	STRETCH (Hold each for 2 mins – omit if you do a class)
	• Alternating back extension (p. 99) • Aeroplanes (p. 100) • Lower body twist (p. 96) • Hover on knees (30 secs) (p. 97) • Leg extensions with twisting crunch (alternating legs) (p. 95) • Kneeling core and balance (right arm, left leg, hold last for 1 min) (p. 98) • Kneeling core and balance (left arm, right leg, hold last for 1 min) (p. 98)	

saturday: fitness

WARM-UP Rowing machine 2 mins, plus 500m sprint	CLASS (Hi-energy, indoor cycle, BodyAttack, step) or **CIRCUIT** ↓		STRETCH
	• Sideways running (3 steps) (p. 106) • Standing biceps curl with barbell (p. 92) • Ice skaters on the spot (p. 107) • Barbell squat (p. 80) • Skipping (1 min) (p. 105) • Standing shoulder press with barbell (p. 91) **FINAL BLAST** Treadmill 5 mins (5.5–6 km/h, level 2)	**ABS** • Fitball crunch (p. 94) • Fitball crunch with twist (p. 94) • Kneeling core and balance (20 each side) (p. 98)	

'in your weights workouts, don't forget to do each pair <u>twice through</u> before moving on to the next pair'

Now the intensity shifts up a gear. Increase your weights by 1–5 kilograms in your weights workouts so that you're groaning by the last couple of reps. Sets and repetitions remain the same. Note that

monday: fitness

WARM-UP Treadmill 5 mins (5–7 km/h, level 4)	CLASS (Indoor cycle, boxing or step) or **CIRCUIT ↓**	ABS	STRETCH
	EXTRA WARM-UP Treadmill interval jogs (no incline): 5 × 30 secs at 7–8 km/h with 30 secs recovery • Push-ups on toes (p. 89) to your max, then finish on your knees (p. 84) • Forward and backward jumps (p. 106) • Triceps bench dips (p. 92) • Sideways running (3 steps) (p. 101) • Standing shoulder press with barbell (p. 91) • Jumping jacks (p. 108) **FINAL BLAST** Cycle 5 mins (aim for 150+ heart rate by end)	• Hover on knees (30 secs) (p. 97) • Fitball crunch (p. 94) • Fitball crunch with twist (p. 94)	

tuesday: toning

WARM-UP Cross trainer with handles 5 mins	CLASS (BodyPump) or **WEIGHTS ↓**	ABS	STRETCH
	• Towel pulls (p. 86) + Fitball squat with dumbbells (p. 81) • Chest press with dumbbells (p. 88) + Static lunge with barbell (15 each leg) (p. 82) • Bent-over fly (p. 85) + Forward power lunge with dumbbells (p. 83) **FINAL BLAST** Treadmill 5 mins (6–8 km/h, level 2)	• Side plank (right 30 secs) (p. 96) • Side plank (left 30 secs) (p. 96) • Hover on toes (30 secs) (p. 97)	

wednesday: fitness

WARM-UP Rowing machine 2 mins, plus 2 × 500m rowing sprints (4 mins rest). Record your time	CLASS (Boxing, indoor cycle, step) or **CIRCUIT ↓**	ABS	STRETCH
	• Walking push-ups on knees with one hand elevated (p. 90) • Basketball jumps (p. 108) • Triceps bench dips (p. 92) • Skipping (1 min) (p. 105) • Ski jumps (p. 107) • Sprints (4 × 15m) **FINAL BLAST** Treadmill 5 mins (6–8 km/h, level 2)	• Leg extensions (p. 95) • Lower body twist (p. 96) • Reverse crunch (p. 94)	

'non-gym-goers, get more creative with your warm-ups: do a flight of stairs ten times; run around two blocks'

you'll be doing the same exercises for *two* weeks, which should help you get more familiar with them. Class-goers should have a go at doing the abs exercises *as well* as the occasional final blast.

thursday: toning

WARM-UP Treadmill 5 mins (6–7 km/h, level 2)	CLASS (BodyPump) or **WEIGHTS** ↓	ABS	STRETCH
	• Dumbbell rows (p. 86) + Step-ups with dumbbells (p. 84) • Chest press with barbell (p. 87) + Sumo squat with barbell (p. 84) • Bent-over fly (p. 85) + Dynamic lunge with light dumbbells (p. 83) **FINAL BLAST** Treadmill 5 mins (6–8 km/h, level 2)	• Crunch (p. 93) • Reverse crunch (p. 94) • Double crunch (p. 95)	

friday: light fitness, core strength and stretch

WARM-UP Cycle 15 mins or treadmill 15 mins (5.5–7 km/h, level 2)	CLASS (Pilates, yoga, BodyBalance, core) or **CIRCUIT** ↓	STRETCH (Hold each for 2 mins — omit if you do a class)
	• Fitball back extension (alternating right and left) (p. 99) • Supported fitball back extension (p. 100) • Fitball crunch with right twist (p. 94) • Fitball crunch with left twist (p. 94) • Leg extensions with twisting crunch (p. 95) • Lower body twist (p. 96) **FINAL BLAST** Treadmill 5 mins (5 km/h, level 2)	

saturday: fitness

WARM-UP Skipping 5 mins, plus cycle 5 mins	CLASS (hi-energy, indoor cycle, BodyAttack, step) or **CIRCUIT** ↓	ABS	STRETCH
	EXTRA WARM-UP Treadmill interval sprints (incline level 1): 5 × 30 secs at 9–10 km/h with 30 secs recovery • Fast low-step running right leg (p. 104) • Fast low-step running left leg (p. 104) • Standing biceps curl with barbell (p. 92) • Forward and backward jumps (p. 106) • Push-ups on toes to your maximum, then finish on your knees (p. 89) • Ice skaters on the spot (p. 107) • Sideways running (5 steps) (p. 106) **FINAL BLAST** Treadmill 5 mins (6–8 km/h, level 2)	• Crunch with right twist (p. 93) • Crunch with left twist (p. 93) • Lower body twist (p. 96)	

'if I've underestimated your fitness here, and you can do more, go for it — don't hold back!'

Congratulations! You have one month under your belt, so now it's time to turn up the heat! Perform the super sets in the toning workouts *three* times through (still for 15 repetitions each) and try to spike your heart rate to 150 BPM several times each session.

monday: fitness

WARM-UP Rowing machine 3 mins plus a 500m sprint (record your time)	CLASS (Boxing, indoor cycle, BodyAttack, step) *or* CIRCUIT ↓	ABS	STRETCH
	EXTRA WARM-UP Treadmill interval sprints: 5 × 30 secs at 7–10 km/h with 30 secs off • Forward and backward jumps (p. 106) • Standing shoulder press with barbell (p. 91) • Skipping (p. 100) 1 min • Dynamic lunge (p. 83) right • Dynamic lunge (p. 83) left • Push-ups on toes to your max, then finish on your knees (p. 89) • Ice skaters on the spot (p. 107) **FINAL BLAST** Treadmill 5 mins (5.5 km/h, level 5)	• Crunch × 100 (*one* set only) (p. 93)	

tuesday: toning

WARM-UP Cross trainer with handles 5 mins	CLASS (Body Pump) *or* WEIGHTS ↓	ABS	STRETCH
	• Bent-over fly (p. 85) + Sumo squat with barbell (p. 84) • Chest press with dumbbells on fitball (p. 88) + Barbell squat (p. 80) • Dumbbell rows (p. 86) + Dynamic lunge with dumbbells (15 each leg) (p. 83) **FINAL BLAST** Treadmill 5 mins (6–8 km/h, level 2)	• Crunch with twist (p. 93) alternating right and left • Hover on knees then toes (p. 97) 30 secs to 1 min • Reverse crunch (p. 94)	

wednesday: fitness

WARM-UP Treadmill 5 mins (5 km/h, level 6)	CLASS (Boxing, indoor cycle, BodyAttack, step) *or* CIRCUIT ↓	ABS	STRETCH
	• Triceps bench dips (p. 92) • Ice skaters on the spot (p. 107) • Baskbetball jumps (p. 108) • Fast low-step running right leg (p. 104) • Fast low-step running left leg (p. 104) • Standing shoulder press with barbell (p. 91) • Ski jumps (p. 107) **FINAL BLAST** Treadmill 5 mins (6–8 km/h, level 2)	• Leg extensions (p. 95) • Lower body twist (p. 96) • Side plank, knees or feet (p. 96) 30 secs each side	

Stick to 20 repetitions for the fitness and abs exercises, but do them *three* times through (except for your 100-crunch abs days — Monday and Saturday). Once again, class-goers should do the abs, *plus* all the final blasts this time.

thursday: toning

WARM-UP Skipping 5 mins	CLASS (BodyPump) *or* **WEIGHTS** ↓	ABS	STRETCH
	• Chest press with barbell (incline bench) (p. 88) + Step-ups with dumbbells (p. 84) • Towel-pulls (p. 86) + Fitball squat with dumbbells (p. 81) • Push-ups on toes (p. 89) + Barbell squat (p. 80) with 5 × 5 bottom halves **FINAL BLAST** Treadmill 5 mins (5.5 km/h, level 6)	• Leg extensions with twist (p. 95) • Supported crunch with medicine ball (p. 93) • Hover (p. 97) 30 secs to 1 min	

friday: light fitness, core strength and stretch

WARM-UP Cycle 15 mins or treadmill 15 mins (5.5–7 km/h, level 2)	CLASS (Pilates, yoga, BodyBalance, core) *or* **CIRCUIT** ↓	STRETCH (Hold each for 2 mins — omit if you do a class)
	• Kneeling core and balance (right arm, left leg, holding last one for 1 min) (p. 98) • Kneeling core and balance (left arm, right leg, holding last one for 1 min) (p. 98) • Kneeling core and balance, with diagonal reach (alternating) (p. 98) • Fitball crunch with twist (alternating right and left) (p. 94) • Fitball crunch with medicine ball (p. 94) • Fitball alternating back extension (p. 99) • Leg extensions (p. 95) **FINAL BLAST** Treadmill 5 mins (5.5 km/h, level 2)	

saturday: fitness

WARM-UP Treadmill 5 mins (7 km/h, level 2)	CLASS (Boxing, indoor cycle, BodyAttack, step) *or* **CIRCUIT** ↓	ABS	STRETCH
	EXTRA WARM-UP Treadmill interval sprints: 10 × 30 secs at 8–10 km/h with 30 secs recovery • Walking push-up, one hand elevated (p. 85) • Forward and backward jumps (p. 106) • Sprints (4 × 15m) • Sideways running (3 steps each way) (p. 106) • Standing biceps curl with barbell (p. 92) • Jumping jacks (p. 108) **FINAL BLAST** Treadmill 5 mins (5 km/h, level 7)	• Fitball crunch × 100, *one* set only — try not to stop! (p. 94)	

You should be pretty fit by now, and the fitter you are the harder you can work, *so go for it*! Aim to spike your heart rate at 150+ several times in the workouts. This week do your fitness circuit only *twice through* (I have added new drills to the beginning) except on Saturday, when you'll do it three times. For weights

monday: fitness

WARM-UP Cross trainer with handles 5 mins	**CLASS** (Boxing, indoor cycle, BodyAttack, step, hi-energy) *or* **CIRCUIT ↓**	**ABS**	STRETCH
	EXTRA WARM-UP Treadmill interval sprints: 10 × 30 secs at 8–10 km/h with 30 secs recovery (once) • Push-ups on toes (p. 89) • Jumping jacks (p. 108) • Standing shoulder press with barbell (light) (p. 91) • Sideways running (3 steps) (p. 106) • Basketball jumps (p. 108) • Ski jumps (p. 107) **FINAL BLAST** Treadmill 5 mins (6–8 km/h, level 3)	• Crunch with right twist (p. 93) • Crunch with left twist (p. 93) • Hover on knees or toes (p. 97) 1 min	

tuesday: toning

WARM-UP Rowing machine 5 mins	**CLASS** (BodyPump, go heavy in squats and back) *or* **WEIGHTS ↓**	**ABS**	STRETCH
	• Chest press with barbell (p. 87) + Sumo squat with barbell (p. 84) • Bent-over fly (p. 85) + Step-ups with medium dumbbells (p. 84) 15 right and 15 left • Walking push-ups with one hand elevated (p. 90) + Fitball hamstring curl (p. 81) **FINAL BLAST** Treadmill 5 mins (8–10 km/h, level 2)	• Leg extensions (p. 95) • Double crunch (p. 95) • Side plank (p. 96) knees or feet, 30 secs each side	

wednesday: fitness

WARM-UP Treadmill 5 mins (8–10 km/h, level 2)	**CLASS** (Boxing, indoor cycle, BodyAttack, step) *or* **CIRCUIT ↓**	**ABS**	STRETCH
	EXTRA WARM-UP Treadmill jog 15 mins (7 km/h, level 2) or walk 15 mins (5 km/h, level 12) • Forward and backward jumps (p. 106) • Ice skaters on the spot (p. 107) • Triceps bench dips (feet elevated) (p. 92) • Skipping (1 min) (p. 105) • Backward power lunge (alternating legs) (p. 83) • Sprints (6 × 15m) **FINAL BLAST** Rowing machine 500m sprint (record your time)	• Supported crunch with medicine ball (p. 93) • Leg extensions with twisting crunch (p. 95) • Lower body twist (p. 96)	

sessions stick to three sets of 15 reps, but you *must* be struggling by the last couple of reps. If you're not puffing, then increase the weight! Do your abs *three* times through (still 20 reps each). Once again, class-goers do the blasts and abs too.

thursday: toning

WARM-UP Cross trainer 5 mins	CLASS (BodyPump, go heavy in chest and lungs) *or* **WEIGHTS ↓**	ABS	STRETCH
	• Towel pulls (p. 86) + Fitball squat with dumbbells (p. 81) • Chest press with dumbbells on fitball (p. 88) + Static lunge with medium barbell (15 each leg) (p. 82) • Dumbbell rows (15 each arm) (p. 80) + Sumo squat with barbell (p. 84) **FINAL BLAST** Treadmill 5 mins (8–10 km/h, level 2)	• Reverse crunch (p. 94) • Fitball crunch (p. 94) • Fitball crunch with twist (alternating right and left) (p. 94)	

friday: light fitness, core strength and stretch

WARM-UP Cycle 15 mins or treadmill 15 mins (5.5–6.5 km/h, level 2)	CLASS (Pilates, yoga, BodyBalance, core) *or* **CIRCUIT ↓**	STRETCH (Hold each for 2 mins – omit if you do a class)
	• Kneeling core and balance (right arm, left leg, holding last one for 1 min) (p. 98) • Kneeling core and balance (left arm, right leg, holding last one for 1 min) (p. 98) • Kneeling core and balance, with diagonal reach (alternating) (p. 98) • Side plank (1 min each on right and left) (p. 96) • Crunch with twist (alternating right and left) (p. 93) • Hover on knees or toes (1 min) (p. 97) • Leg extensions (p. 95) • Reverse crunch (p. 94) **FINAL BLAST** Treadmill 5 mins (5.5–6.5 km/h, level 2)	

saturday: fitness

WARM-UP Treadmill 5 mins (8–10 km/h, level 2)	CLASS (Boxing, indoor cycle, BodyAttack, step) *or* **CIRCUIT ↓**	STRETCH
	EXTRA WARM-UP Treadmill interval sprints: 10 × 30 secs at 8–10 km/h with 30 secs recovery • Walking push-ups with one hand elevated (p. 90) + Sprints (4 × 15m) • Dynamic lunge right (p. 83) + Sprints (4 × 15m) • Dynamic lunge left (p. 83) + Sprints (4 × 15m) • Standing biceps curl with barbell (p. 92) + Sprints (4 × 15m) • Ice skaters on the spot (p. 107) + Sprints (4 × 15m) • Triceps bench dips (p. 92) + Sprints (4 × 15m) • Take a 3-min breather then go again, twice more **FINAL BLAST** Cross trainer 5 mins	

'on saturday I want you to do the circuit <u>three</u> times!'

By now, some of you may have already reached your target weight, especially if your plan was to lose 5–10 kilos. For those who still have more to lose, seek and destroy! The new fitter, stronger, healthier, sexier you must do *three* sets of 20 reps in your circuits and abs, and *three* sets of 15 reps in your weights

monday: fitness

WARM-UP Cross trainer 5 mins	CLASS (Boxing, indoor cycle, BodyAttack, step, hi-energy) *or* CIRCUIT ↓	ABS	STRETCH
	• Skipping 1 min + Sprints (4 × 15m) • Shoulder press + Sprints (4 × 15m) • Basketball jumps + Sprints (4 × 15m) • Triceps bench dips + Sprints (4 × 15m) • Squat jumps + Sprints (4 × 15m) • Take a 2-min breather then go again, twice more **FINAL BLAST** Treadmill 5 mins (6 km/h, level 6)	• Crunch × 150 (once)	

tuesday: toning

WARM-UP Cross trainer with handles 5 mins	CLASS (BodyPump, go heavy in squats, back and lunges) *or* WEIGHTS ↓	ABS	STRETCH
	• Towel pulls + Step-ups (high bench) with dumbbells (15 each leg) • Chest press with dumbbells + Barbell squat • Dumbbell rows (15 each arm) + Fitball hamstring curl **FINAL BLAST** Treadmill 5 mins (8–10 km/h, level 2)	• Crunch with right twist • Crunch with left twist • Reverse crunch	

wednesday: fitness

WARM-UP Rowing machine 3 mins plus 500m sprint (record your time)	CLASS (hi-energy, boxing, indoor cycle, BodyAttack, step) *or* CIRCUIT ↓	ABS	STRETCH
	EXTRA WARM-UP Treadmill jog 20 mins (8–10 km/h, level 2), 10 mins at 8–10 km/h, *plus* 10 mins at 5.5 km/h (level 12) • Walking push-ups with one hand elevated • Forward and backward jumps • Standing shoulder press with barbell • Ice skaters on the spot • Backward power lunge (20 each leg) • Sideways running (5 steps) **FINAL BLAST** Cycle 5 mins	• Supported crunch with medicine ball • Supported crunch with medicine ball with twist • Supported crunch (no ball)	

workouts. Your target is to spike your heart rate at 150+ several times. As usual, repeat these exercises for two weeks, and class-goers do blasts and abs.

thursday: toning

WARM-UP Cross trainer 5 mins	CLASS (BodyPump) or **WEIGHTS ↓**	ABS	STRETCH
	• Chest press with dumbbells on fitball + Fitball squat with dumbbells (narrow stance) • Dumbbell rows + Forward power lunge with dumbbells (15 each leg) • Standing shoulder press with dumbbells + Sumo squat with barbell **FINAL BLAST** Treadmill 5 mins (8–10 km/h, level 2)	• Leg extension with twisting crunch • Hover on toes 1 min • Fitball crunch	

friday: light fitness, core strength and stretch

WARM-UP Cycle 15 mins (aim for 150+ heart rate by end)	CLASS (Pilates, yoga, BodyBalance, core) or **CIRCUIT ↓**	STRETCH (Hold each for 2 mins – omit if you do a class)
	• Leg extension with twist • Hover on knees or toes (hold for one 1 min) • Alternating back extension • Aeroplanes • Crunches × 10 with 10-sec hold at top • Reverse crunches × 10 with 5-sec hold at top **FINAL BLAST** Treadmill 5 mins (5.5 km/h, level 2)	

saturday: fitness

WARM-UP Skipping 5 mins	CLASS (Running club, hi-energy, boxing, indoor cycle, BodyAttack, step) or **CIRCUIT ↓**	ABS	STRETCH
	• Push-ups on toes + Sprints (4 × 15m) • Sideways running (3 steps) + Sprints (4 × 15m) • Triceps bench dips (feet elevated) + Sprints (4 × 15m) • Forward and backward jumps + Sprints (4 × 15m) • Standing biceps curl with barbell + Sprints (4 × 15m) • Forward power lunge (alternating legs) + Sprints (4 × 15m) • Take a 1-min breather then go again, twice more **FINAL BLAST** Treadmill 10 mins (5.5 km/h, level 6)	• Fitball crunch • Fitball crunch with right twist • Fitball crunch with left twist • Lower body twist	

'because you should really know your exercises by now,
I don't give you page references to look them up'

This is it. It's been a long time in the making, but you've arrived at the final workouts! On your fitness days, do three sets of 20 reps and on your toning days, three sets of 15 reps, but keep increasing the weights so that your last couple of reps are real groaners! For your abs, do *three* sets of 20 reps.

monday: fitness

WARM-UP Rowing machine 3 mins plus 500m sprint	CLASS (Boxing, indoor cycle, BodyAttack, step) or **CIRCUIT** ↓	ABS	STRETCH
	• Skipping rope (1 min) + Sprints (4 × 15m) • Push-ups on toes + Sprints (4 × 15m) • Dynamic lunge (right) + Sprints (6 × 15m) • Dynamic lunge (left) + Sprints (8 × 15m) • Shoulder press with barbell + Sprints (10 × 15m) • Take a 2-min breather then go again, twice more **FINAL BLAST** Cross trainer 5 mins	• Crunch × 200 (I mean it! Break them into sets of 20 reps if it helps)	

tuesday: toning

WARM-UP Treadmill 5 mins (8–10 km/h, level 2)	CLASS (BodyPump) or **WEIGHTS** ↓	ABS	STRETCH
	• Towel pulls + Step-ups with dumbbells • Chest press with dumbbells (heavy) + Fitball hamstring curl • Dumbbells row (15 each arm) + Forward power lunge with dumbbells (15 each leg) **FINAL BLAST** Cycle 5 mins (aim for 160+ heart rate by the end)	• Leg extensions with twisting crunch • Crunch with right twist holding medicine ball • Crunch with left twist holding medicine ball • Reverse crunch	

wednesday: fitness

WARM-UP Cross trainer 5 mins plus rowing machine 500m sprint (beat your time!)	CLASS (Boxing, indoor cycle, BodyAttack, step) or **CIRCUIT** ↓	ABS	STRETCH
	EXTRA WARM-UP Treadmill interval sprints: 10 × 30 secs at 8–12 km/h with 30-sec recovery (once) • Forward and backward jumps • Triceps bench dips • Over-the-fence jumps • Push-ups on toes • Basketball jumps • Ice skaters on the spot **FINAL BLAST** Treadmill 5 mins (8–10 km/h)	• Double crunch • Lower body twist • Leg extensions	

'do today's circuit <u>four times</u> through, just because you can!'

Your heart rate should be high enough so that you are breathless for most of the workout. Beat your best times in *all* your warm-ups! Class-goers do warm-ups, abs *and* final blasts. This is the *home straight* – get mad, get mean, get macho!

thursday: toning

WARM-UP Treadmill 5 mins (8–10 km/h)	CLASS (BodyPump) *or* **WEIGHTS** ↓	ABS	STRETCH
	• Towel pulls + Fitball squat with dumbbells (heavy) with 5 × 8 bottom halves • Dumbbell rows + Dynamic lunge with medium dumbbells (15 each leg) • Chest press with barbell (flat bench) + Squat with barbell **FINAL BLAST** Rowing machine 5 mins	• Leg extensions + Crunch with twist (alternating right and left) • Hover on toes (1 min) • Fitball crunch with medicine ball	

friday: light fitness, core strength and stretch

WARM-UP Cycle 15 mins (aim for 150+ heart rate by end)	CLASS (Pilates, yoga, BodyBalance, core) *or* **CIRCUIT** ↓	STRETCH (Hold each for 2 mins – omit if you do a class)
	• Fitball alternating back extension • Hand hover (hold for 1 min) • Alternating back extension • Aeroplanes • Crunches × 10 with 10-sec pause at the top • Reverse crunches × 10 with 5-sec pause at top **FINAL BLAST** Treadmill 5 mins (5.5–6 km/h, level 2)	

saturday: fitness

WARM-UP Skipping 5 mins	CLASS (BodyPump, hi-energy, boxing, indoor cycle, BodyAttack, step) *or* **CIRCUIT** ↓	ABS	STRETCH
	• Ski jumps • Walking push-ups with one hand elevated • Ice skaters on the spot • Push-ups on toes • Over-the-fence jumps • Sideways running (5 steps) • Sprints (8 × 15m) **FINAL BLAST** Treadmill 5 mins (5 km/h, level 15)	• Fitball crunch × 150 (once only)	

'over-the-fence jumps are tough, but you can do them now'

what now?

Congratulations! You have done what so many can only dream of. You have completed a full three months of training. I have no doubt that you experienced the good, the bad and the downright ugly! But you are here, you survived and now you know what you are capable of — far more than you ever thought, right?

So let's talk weight. How much have you lost? And how much more do you have to lose? For those of you who have nailed your goal weight, no doubt you are feeling invincible! Some of you may have even shifted the goal posts – many of my clients do when they get to this point. Instead of aiming for a size 14 they are now eyeing off size 12. That's brilliant, and I encourage you to go for it. It may mean repeating another few weeks of workouts, but by now you will be a savvy exerciser, and you'll know how long and how hard you need to go to burn the calories.

For those of you who are out to drop fifty or more kilos, you should be at or just past your halfway mark. Now do the full twelve weeks of workouts again, obviously upping the intensity to match and challenge your current fitness. I know you can do it — the weight you have already lost is proof of that. If you're out to lose more than fifty kilos, six months is a realistic timeline.

This is where you do not drop the ball and leave the game. That may have been where you took a wrong turn last time — remember, you are doing things differently this time.

Whether you are at your goal weight or at the halfway point, there are a few things that will never change:

- **you are an exerciser** — it's who you are. You clean your teeth, you make you bed, you train. You will do an hour's exercise six days a week and look forward to it because you know how fantastic it makes you feel. You will always take the stairs instead of the lift and walk instead of taking the car because you know that every bit of informal exercise helps — and because it just feels right.
- **you are careful with what you eat** — you will always make the smart choices, you will always know where you are with your calorie intake and you will keep workin' that kitchen to become a great low-calorie chef!
- **you set yourself up for success** by every day *choosing* to train hard and eat well.

This is what you will do. And the reward? A happier, healthier, sexier you! One hundred per cent worth it!

'this is where you do not drop the ball and leave the game — remember, you are doing things differently this time'

get *cooking!*

11
nutrition

'losing weight always comes down to what you put in your mouth — end of story!'

CHANCES ARE IF YOU ARE OVERWEIGHT that you are food-obsessed. You may even be addicted to food. Tough call, I know, but check in with yourself. How much of your day do you spend eating? Add to this the time you spend preparing food or getting yourself to places where you can buy or eat food. Then add the time that you are thinking and talking about food. If you've got quite a few hours totalled up then clearly you have an *emotional* relationship to food.

An emotional relationship to food is a consistent pattern with overeaters. If you find yourself turning to food when you're stressed or unhappy, or if eating huge quantities of calorie-dense junk is something you associate with reward, celebration and good times, then you've moved away from the principle of food for sustenance. Food for you has come to mean something different.

There's nothing new about using food as a celebration. We've been doing it for centuries, when special occasions were marked by feasting that sometimes went on for days. The difference is that in the modern age, this 'celebration' food is available *every day* and *everywhere*. Nowadays, it doesn't have to be a special occasion for us to hoe into a five-course meal — any day that ends in a 'y' will do just fine!

junk food

Readily available junk food and our ever-increasing desire to eat it have resulted in an explosion of fast-food outlets, causing the rate of obesity in the population to skyrocket. Compare our eating habits to those of other Western countries, and then compare the availability of calorie-dense takeaway outlets and you'll see why France, Italy or any other country that has resisted the influx doesn't have the same obesity issues that we have.

Because fast-food manufacturers work in huge volumes, their products are cheaper — it's no coincidence that obesity is more prevalent in less affluent areas. Yet we've *all* been fooled into thinking that it's actually cheaper to eat fast food than wholefood. It isn't. We've also been brainwashed to believe that it's more convenient, which we sometimes use as an excuse to make poor food choices: 'I haven't got time to cook. I'll just grab some takeaway.' **I guarantee you can make a healthy, nutritious meal in less than 20 minutes, and that it costs a quarter of the price of a fast-food equivalent.**

We must remember, though, that fast food is not the only junk food. Let's take a walk around your average supermarket and see what else qualifies, starting with the first meal of the day — breakfast. Around 80 per cent of breakfast cereals can be classified as junk, despite claims for added vitamins, as they generally include loads of added sugar. And let's not forget sodium (salt). Did you know that there is a cereal marketed to children which has more sodium per serve than a packet of chips?!

My classification of junk food also includes all those ready-made pies and other dishes in the frozen-food section, and the entire cakes and biscuits section. Add to the list soft drinks, cordials and all the potato chips and snacks that are cleverly located next to them. It also includes most of the ready-made sauces and packets of just-add-water slop. Ditto the entire

'let me tell you, there are entire shopping aisles you must never visit again if you are to reach your goal'

confectionary section, most of the canned fruits, dips, white breads, margarines and all those 'snacks in a box'.

Don't get sucked into the 'low-fat' label, either. **If it's low fat, then the nutritional label should prove it to you beyond doubt.** Low-fat foods can still be high in calories if they contain a lot of sugars (carbohydrates). The quickest way to check their suitability is to read the calorie content — but *beware*! When you check the number of calories *per serve*, make sure that the serve is what you would normally eat, and not some paltry offering.

The biggest problem, however, with a lot of these sorts of low-fat, low-calorie foods is that they're often low in nutritional value as well and, being ready-made, prevent you learning about food preparation. **Don't let the food companies dumb you down!** Let me tell you, there are *entire shopping aisles* you must *never* visit again if you are to reach your goal.

Now if that sounds scary, hear this, because it may well be the most important thing you'll read. While exercise will do *amazing* things for your mind, your body and your spirit, losing weight will always come down to what you put in your mouth! *End of story!*

If I had two clients, one of whom refused to eat well and ate whatever she liked whenever she liked, but I trained her like a demon every day, and another who did no exercise but tidied up her diet so that she had a weekly calorie deficit, the non-exerciser would lose the most weight.

Of course the best scenario is the double-whammy approach:

- Good nutrition + exercise =
  FAST RESULTS!
- Fast results =
  BETTER MOTIVATION
- Better motivation =
  EVEN FASTER RESULTS!

what's *really* in your food?

Now, I'm no chemist, but a little bit of science helps to explain why food does what it does, and why some foods lead us to needing a post-code for our butts while others don't.

We have four major sources of energy: protein, carbohydrates, fats and alcohol. Yes, alcohol. You need to understand the role of *all* the energy sources you put into your body, and although strictly speaking alcohol is just another carbohydrate (it's not even a food by definition, because it doesn't supply any micro-nutrients, such as vitamins and minerals), it's one that is omnipresent in the modern era and is totally relevant in the weight-loss debate.

You need to understand the distinction between nutrient-dense and calorie-dense foods. Nutrient-dense foods generally contain fewer calories so we can eat more of them. These are what we call wholefoods and include unprocessed meat, poultry, fish, fruit, vegetables and grains that have been refined as little as possible (such as in wholegrain bread). Be aware, though, that not all wholefoods are low

food type	calories (kilojoules) per gram
Carbohydrates (fruit, vegetables, grains)	3.8 (16)
Protein (nuts, eggs, chicken, beef etc.)	4.0 (17)
Fat (oil, butter, milk, cheese)	8.8 (37)
Alcohol	6.4 (27)

in calories, which is why you can *still* be overweight with a healthy diet. A great example of this is an avocado, which is a whopping 500 calories!

Calorie-dense foods generally have fewer nutrients and are often higher in fat or sugar, or both. At the top end are chips, ice-cream, chocolate, burgers, hot dogs, etc., most containing the nutritional value of a sock.

carbohydrates

Carbohydrates would have to be one of the most contentious, confusing and over-analysed energy sources in our food. This is all you need to understand:

- Carbohydrates are found in most foods.
- Our bodies use carbohydrates to make glucose, which gives us energy and allows our brains to function properly.
- Because our bodies use *all* carbs for fuel, it's up to us to choose ones that are high in nutrients and low in calories, i.e. wholefoods.

low-GI carbohydrates

The GI (glycemic index) is a measure of how fast carbohydrates enter the bloodstream. Low GI is rated at 55 or less; medium GI is 56–69; and high GI is 70 or more. High-GI foods are not necessarily bad, in fact they are fantastic if you are about to run a race and need a quick hit of energy. However, diabetics and weight-loss candidates should stick to low and, occasionally, medium GI. It's no coincidence that unrefined wholefoods are generally low GI.

carbohydrate-rich wholefoods

- brown/basmati rice
- fruit & vegetables
- honey
- milk
- minimally processed cereals (bran, muesli, oats)
- rice noodles
- wholemeal pasta & bread

'when it comes to food, information is power'

'if your primary goal is to lose weight, then your primary concern should be the number of calories you eat'

protein

Protein is essential for the building and repair of all body tissue, including skin, blood, hair and organs. It is also the primary element of muscle, so protein is crucial for the exercisers out there (by which I mean *everyone*, of course). Protein is found in meat, fish, dairy products, seeds, nuts and legumes. It makes you feel full, which can prevent overeating, and it's really easy to dish out the right portion size (half a breast of chicken, a palm-sized piece of steak). Just make sure you remove all the fat.

protein shakes

Protein shakes are an excellent supplement if you are training hard because they assist with muscle recovery. I use them to top up my protein levels if I don't feel like eating meat for every meal or if I'm in a rush to get to work. They're also great if I am about to go out for a really late dinner and need to put something in my tummy (it means I'm less likely to pig out at dinner, too). Protein shakes can also be very useful for vegetarians.

fats

Fats or fatty acids are an important energy source and are required for healthy skin and some body functions. Fats should make up around 20–30 per cent of our daily calorie intake, but we need to be careful to eat the right kind of fats.

All fats are high in calories. Watch out for nuts in particular. While they are nutritious, they're also calorie-dense. Dieticians recommend eating only ten almonds as a snack, but are *they* nuts? Who stops at ten? I never recommend them for snacks — they're just too tempting. I'd rather use them in my cooking or scatter them in a salad — that way I eat less. Likewise avocadoes and olive oil — when it comes to storing calories, your body does not differentiate between good and bad fats.

protein-rich wholefoods
- lean red meats (beef, kangaroo, lamb)
- lean poultry (chicken, quail)
- fish & shellfish
- eggs
- milk, cheese, yoghurt
- tofu products
- legumes (beans, peas, chickpeas, lentils, peanuts)
- nuts & seeds (walnuts, almonds, pumpkin seeds, sunflower seeds)

THE GOOD GUYS	
Mono-unsaturated fats are easily used as fuel and help decrease cholesterol levels.	Olive oil, canola oil, peanut oil, avocado, almonds, peanuts, cashews, macadamias, hazelnuts, pecans, eggs
Polyunsaturated fats (found in oily fish and plant food) include omega-3 and omega-6, which are essential fatty acids because they're crucial to our health but our bodies can't make them. Omega-3 has been shown to help prevent heart disease, so is very popular right now.	**Omega-6**: eggs, cereals, poultry, pine nuts, seeds, vegetable oil (e.g. sunflower, safflower, soybean, corn) **Omega-3**: salmon, sardines, tuna, mackerel, anchovies, trout, herring, linseed oil, walnuts, eggs
THE BAD GUYS	
Trans-fats (also called hydrogenated fats) are polyunsaturates that have been treated so they remain solid at room temperature — they're used extensively in foods (always check the label) and are crap.	Chips, pastries, doughnuts, biscuits, muffins, cakes, pies, margarine
Saturated fats (found in meat and dairy products) are the bad guys — they're more readily stored as body fat and less easily used as fuel. They also raise blood cholesterol levels.	Meat fat, chicken fat, butter, full-fat milk/yoghurt, cream, cheese, coconut milk, palm oil, deep-fried fast food

alcohol

Only your liver can metabolise alcohol, and while it's busy doing that any excess alcohol floats around in your bloodstream messing up other organs (like your brain!) Your body breaks down foods *preferentially*, and it will always metabolise alcohol first, then carbohydrates, followed by fats and, as a last resort, protein. This sounds okay, until you remember that last night you were chowing down on potato wedges with sour cream and cashew nuts while you slurped a few beers! And then you went and had dinner with a few more drinks to boot! Now your body will be using the alcohol to fuel itself before it uses the food, so guess where all that food will go? Storage, anyone?

The other thing with alcohol, of course, is that we tend to get pissed and make dumb food choices that can ruin days of careful exercise and nutrition. Alcohol is *evil* for weight loss.

get organised

I cannot overstate the impact of your diet on your weight. Food occupies a much larger part of your life than exercise ever will. Work it out — you train for an hour, six days a week. That's six hours. You'll spend a significant percentage of the other 162 hours organising yourself for, preparing, being tempted by or eating food. So always be guided by the Number One rule: **what goes into your mouth will make the most difference.**

To start eating right you need to surround yourself with high-quality wholefood and be well organised in the kitchen. This means your kitchen will need a significant makeover and you'll need to say goodbye to some old friends. You know the ones: the chocolate sauces, the biscuits (just in case we have visitors — yeah, sure, girlfriend!), the dumb breakfast cereals, the 30-litre bottles of soft drink.

Here's what to do. Go outside and get your wheelie rubbish bin. Wheel it into your kitchen and put it in the middle of the room with the lid open. Starting at the pantry and working your way around the entire kitchen, grab any of the unhealthy crap and launch it *straight into the bin.* As you do, shout 'Get the hell out of my life — I'm *over* you holding me back!'

If you have to stop and think about a particular item for more than 5 seconds, then throw it away anyway for wasting your time. If you sample any of them, then please give yourself a slap across the face from me and read 'Get Real' again! And no, don't give me the old 'but it's such a waste . . .' Let me tell you what a waste is. A waste is having spent the last ten or twenty years of your life with a weight issue that has been hanging around your neck and dragging you down, down, down. A waste is missing out on the fabulous life that is rightfully yours! You deserve more, more, more!

Next, take a trip to the supermarket and re-stock your fridge, freezer and pantry with The Good Stuff. I've made shopping lists for you in the next chapter. This way you'll beat your instincts at their own game by surrounding yourself with food that'll make you *slim*, not food that'll make you *fat*. You are taking control now.

John's heart-warming story

In *The Biggest Loser* we had an older bloke named John who came into the house with a severe heart condition, so severe that his cardiologist banned him from doing any exercise apart from walking for a maximum of 30 minutes three times a day, and even then he wasn't allowed to let his heart rate go above 100 beats per minute (about 57 per cent of his maximum heart rate). He was put on a strict wholefood diet and he walked for half an hour three times a day. After the first ten days John had lost over 10 kilos! He went on to lose more weight, got fitter and was eventually given clearance to do any exercise he wished! Truly one of the most incredible turnarounds I've ever witnessed.

cook the right stuff

Just as you are now an exerciser, you are now a cook. There is no way on this planet that you can accelerate yourself to lean and mean unless you put in some time in the kitchen. **Not only is cooking easy, it also makes you take responsibility for your own nutrition, and that is an important step towards taking responsibility for your own body.** And if you have children, you'll know that this will be one of the best gifts you can give them. This is a long-term gift, not a short-term quick-fix. And you can even get them involved in the cooking process.

My approach to cooking is to keep it simple, and you'll notice that the recipes in Chapter 15 reflect just that. I don't think too many of us have got time during the week to chuck a Gordon Ramsay, so the meals are quick and simple with a minimum of ingredients. For some, I've also included a fancier variation that you might want to try on the weekend, or when you've got more time to spend in the kitchen. It's a good idea to occasionally cook more than you need so that you have a couple of extra serves to freeze or have for lunch the next day.

vegetables

When you open the fridge or pantry door you want to be see a host of fresh vegetables:

think a colourful array of zucchini, carrots, capsicum, asparagus, cauliflower and sweet potatoes.

Vegetables really are the stuff of life. They give your body the nutrients and vitamins it needs. They are full of flavour and have amazing properties (consider cruciferous vegies like broccoli, cauliflower and spinach — they help prevent cancer!) Think about it. When you've gone back for that second helping of cheesecake, how do you feel afterwards? Bloated? A bit sick? You betcha! That's because your body is trying to reject it, because it knows

'there is no way that you can accelerate yourself to lean and mean unless you put in some time in the kitchen'

that it is poisonous to the wonderful mixture of molecules and particles that make up our amazing bodies — your body — the one that you love. Remember?

The other big plus with vegetables is that they are low in calories, so you can eat lots and lots of them without going over your daily calorie limit. How does five asparagus spears, two sliced carrots, a floret of broccoli, a cup of spinach and a couple of yellow squash sound? Enough to complement your marinated chicken breast? That's an amazing plate of vegetables, but it's only 120 calories.

fruit

I think of fruit as nature's lollies. Fruit comes in an amazing variety of colours, sizes and flavours, and adds that bit of sweetness to your life. It is a far better option than a chocolate bar or sugary fizzy drink, that's for sure. Throw a couple of apples into your bag when you leave the house and you've got the perfect snack to get you through the day — you can even eat the packaging!

Fruit is typically high in vitamins as well as fibre and antioxidants, so it helps keep your digestive system in tip-top condition.

Fruit is at its best when it is in season. At this time it's packed with the most flavour, the highest concentration of nutrients, and it's at its cheapest. So experiment with different fruit throughout the year. I like to have some at breakfast and as snacks, but I am also a big fan of fruit in salads.

meat

In the Western world, our diet tends to be largely meat-based. This is not good for you, for the planet or the animals. Meat production is among the least efficient uses of agricultural land, while intensive farming methods means that animal welfare can often be compromised. While meat has a part to play in your diet, and offers important nutritional elements, we need to get smarter about our meat choices and dial back on the amount we eat.

It may take a bit of getting used to, but your new diet is not going to be primarily meat-based. Vegetables are going to form the largest proportion of your diet from now on. Your new approach to meat is to use it almost as a garnish — smaller portions, around 150–200 grams a serve, but well prepared with delicious homemade marinades or spicy toppings.

When meat does feature, it's going to be the leaner varieties and cuts. Some red meat and poultry is good for you, but you want to limit the fat content. That's why I favour things like chicken breast and kangaroo — low fat, high in nutrients and, of course, tasty! Whenever possible, you should choose organic, free-range meat. Not only is this meat free of chemicals and preservatives, it is a much more mindful way of raising animals. It may be a little more expensive (though not as much as you might think), but as you are eating less meat, it makes sense to up the quality.

*'think about what you're going to eat,
and when you're going to eat it, then do
whatever is necessary to make it happen'*

fish

Fish is a brilliant source of protein. Your muscles need protein to develop and grow strong, so you should be getting fish into your diet to aid your exercise — and because it tastes great.

One of the other main nutritional benefits of fish is that it contains omega-3 fatty acids. This compound is really important for healthy brain function, and is thought to help prevent diseases like Alzheimer's and dementia. It also plays a role in the production of serotonin, the brain's 'happy-making' chemical.

I love the sheer variety of tastes and textures that fish and seafood offer, from the sweet globules of scallops to the firm, pink loveliness of a salmon fillet. However, **you need to ensure that your fish comes from a sustainable source**, as many fish populations are in decline from overfishing. Ask your local fishmonger and regularly check the Australian Marine Conservation Society's Sustainable Seafood Guide.

nuts, grains and seeds

Nuts, grains and seeds can sprinkle a little bit of magic into a dish. We don't use a lot of them, as they can be high in fat (particularly nuts), but their taste and nutritional benefits make them great to have in your pantry.

These ingredients are important providers of fibre, which helps your digestive system, and zinc, which is a mineral that plays an essential role in more than 300 physiological processes in your body!

The key with all of these types of food is to buy unadulterated varieties. It should just be the grain or the nut in that packet — no added salt, sugar or preservatives.

dairy

Including such tasty delights as yoghurt, milk and cheese, dairy products also have a key part to play in your new diet. Like meat, they won't tend to be front and centre too often (we've already established that vegetables are gonna fill that particular role), but let's face it, a life without cheese is pretty dull!

However, as with all the food we put in our mouths, it's about making the right choices. Lower calorie cheeses like ricotta and fetta feature often in my recipes, while yoghurt should always be natural and biodynamic, rather than the processed sugary variety which has a lot more calories and fewer nutrients.

Two of the biggest benefits we get from dairy products are protein and calcium. The former helps your muscles and the latter your bones.

control your portions

Most people are overweight because they ingest too many calories, too much food — more food than their bodies actually need. Sure, there can be issues around hormones, prescription drugs, etc., but for the most part people simply *eat too much*.

Take a long, hard look at your portions. There's a good chance you are eating twice as much as you need. You may have been eating hefty portions for so long that you don't even realise *how* big they are. Yes, cutting them down is going to be a little uncomfortable at first. You've trained your stomach to expect *way* more than it needs, so it's probably going to let you know how it feels about the new portions. But you won't die! You will still be able to fill your belly and keep the hunger at bay, but it will be with nutrient-dense, low-calorie wholefoods rather than those with zero nutrients and a gazillion calories.

Here are some smart rules to help you reduce portions:

- Use smaller plates.
- Never go back for seconds. They never taste as good, and you don't need them.
- Never finish off anyone else's food.
- Never eat while you are cooking.

Remember the Seven-Day Food Diary I asked you to keep in Chapter 4? This should have given you a handle on the amount of food

The day I met Michelle I was at rock-bottom. I had been battling my weight for years. I hated looking in the mirror, I felt embarrassed to go out and I was miserable all the time. I knew I had to do something or would face the rest of my life feeling like this. This time I felt absolutely ready, and it was very different to how I'd felt in the past.

Michelle was very straight with me, which was confronting but quite refreshing. She had me 'get real' about my life and what I'd been doing to hold myself back. For the first time in my life, I was completely honest about my eating habits and it felt good. Michelle taught me about 'calories in and calories out' and set up a tough training schedule for me. I think the biggest thing I learnt was that I had to *choose* to eat well and exercise – that it's my responsibility.

I lost 5 kilos in the first ten days – I was so motivated. For the first time I felt like I was in control.

It's been six months, now, since I first met Michelle and I have lost a total of 36 kilos. I am the happiest I have been in all my adult life!

Caroline, 32

you are eating. To work out the calories, you would have needed to weigh food and read the labels on tins and packets. Now, before you start worrying about having to measure and weigh your portions for the rest of your life, don't panic. All I'm asking is that you keep a detailed food diary while you're doing your twelve-week training program. You may not keep a food diary forever, but you will always keep a mental tally of your calories. Within the first week or so you'll know a reasonable-sized portion just by looking at it, but check every couple of weeks that your portions haven't crept up.

Your portions will depend on your calorie quota per day, which in turn depends on your gender and weight (see page 154), but in general, use the following as a guide:

your daily calorie quotas

WOMEN
- 3 meals each ×
  350 cal (1470 kJ)
- 1–2 snacks each ×
  150 cal (630 kJ)
  total = 1350 cal (5670 kJ)

MEN
- 3 meals each ×
  400 cal (1680 kJ)
- 1–2 snacks each ×
  200 cal (840 kJ)
  total = 1600 cal (6720 kJ)

eat regularly

Stop playing games with yourself. You know the ones: 'Well, I've hardly eaten all day so now I can gorge myself' or 'So, if I skip breakfast and only have an apple for lunch then I can tuck into a smorgasbord and a crate of beer'. Before you know it, you'll have taken in more calories than if you'd eaten breakfast and lunch put together. So, give up the games. They do not work, and they will leave you feeling tired and angry with yourself.

From now on you will eat breakfast, lunch *and* dinner. You will have a snack during the day only if you need the energy and you will no longer binge at night. Your focus will be on eating more during the day when you need it and less at night.

- eat like a **king** for breakfast
- eat like a **prince** for lunch
- eat like a **pauper** for dinner

Eat your evening meal as early as you can, brush your teeth, pull the plug, *game over*! Okay, I get that you have a life. Stuff comes up like birthdays, events and parties. I get it. However, it's what you do 95 per cent of the time that counts. The *occasional* Saturday night here or there won't make a difference if you are rockin' on clean the rest of the time.

Is it really 'low-fat'?

Any smart city girl (or boy) knows that the way to get the best food on an airline, and to get it before everyone else, is to put yourself down for special dietary requirements. So naturally I've always insisted on a low-fat meal to keep my calorie count down. On one particularly long flight Billy and I decided to kill some time with a calorie-count comparison of our meals. He got the everyday stuff.

We estimated that my 'low-fat' meal (a banana, OJ, low-fat cereal, skim milk and a berry bar) totalled around 552 calories with 9.6 grams of fat – without tea or coffee. Now that's a fair-dinkum brekkie (it was the 'healthy' bar that blew it at 250 calories). I'd normally be shooting for 350 to 450 tops, so I chucked the bar and stayed within my limit.

Billy got his meal, cereal and toast complete with full-cream milk and butter, and it came in at 520 calories, 32 calories *less* than mine! The message? Unless you take responsibility for your own food, *you don't have a chance*. Calorie-dense food is everywhere, because it tastes good and the food companies know that. They've designed it to give your tastebuds instant gratification when it makes contact, never mind that you feel like you've swallowed a house brick afterwards.

forget low fat!

Okay, here we go – deep breath. *If you want to lose weight quickly, forget low fat* (collective gasp of horror from the entire Western world). Let me qualify that just a little before the avalanche of hate mail arrives from the food companies. **If your primary goal is to lose weight, your primary concern should be the number of calories you eat.** Now this doesn't mean you can eat crap provided you stay within your daily calorie count, because crap isn't nutritious and won't keep your body functioning properly. What it means is that when you're standing in the supermarket squinting at the nutritional analysis label on the side of a tub of yoghurt, the first thing you should look at is the calorie (kilojoule) content per serving. After that, check out the fats, sugars etc. The calorie content is inextricably linked to the fat content anyway: more fat equals more calories.

We've been told for decades that we should buy 'lite', or 'low fat', or 'fat free'. Now we're being told to buy 'low carb'. At the end of the day, fat is *not* the most important factor in making your weight-loss food choices. What have we got to show for twenty years of low-fat eating? The Obesity Epidemic. That's because, even though the foods available to us are low in fat, they are still frequently high in calories, and our 'inner Labrador' has always read 'low fat' as 'eat more' anyway. And trust me, there are some shocks out there with products that are purporting to be low fat. Once again, *know your calories*.

reduce alcohol intake

Speaking from experience, if there's one thing that kills your willpower, it's alcohol. Get a few drinks into you and suddenly all that inner strength goes down the toilet, often along with the booze. On top of that, alcohol is full of calories and is mostly consumed at night when you should be taking in fewer calories, not more. Then when you train the next day (and you *will* train with a hangover – you play, you pay) your body uses the alcohol first for energy, which sounds good on the face of it, until you remember that you didn't exactly reach for a fruit salad last night either. It was more like cheese, crackers, chips, dips and, oh yeah, the kebab at 3 a.m. **Limit alcohol to two nights a week and keep it in check. For faster results, cut it out completely.**

snack right

As you've learned in Chapter 9, your body will go into panic mode if you don't eat regularly, and will begin to store energy (fat) if it suspects there's a chance of starvation. Healthy snacks prevent this, and also stop you making dumb food choices because you're too hungry to think straight. However, don't feel that you have to snack between meals – if you're *really* not hungry, wait until your next meal.

healthy snacks

- 1 × 200 g tub low-cal plain yoghurt with a couple of strawberries (120 cals / 504 kJ)
- 2 celery sticks spread with 3 tablespoons low-cal ricotta cheese (120 cals / 504 kJ)
- 10 snow peas, 10 sugar snap peas and 10 green beans (50 cals / 210 kJ)
- 3 slices apple (1 cm thick) topped with 1 tablespoon low-cal ricotta cheese and a mint leaf (120 cals / 504 kJ)
- 1 × 150 g punnet blueberries (85 cals / 357 kJ) (way cheaper than a coffee and a muffin, and so much better for you!)
- 1 med raw carrot (140 g) munched and dipped in 3 tablespoons low-cal ricotta cheese (120 cals / 504 kJ)
- 1 × 250 g punnet strawberries (50 cals / 210 kJ)
- 3 wheat crackers spread with Vegemite (150 cals / 630 kJ)
- 6 small rice crackers each with ½ tablespoon low-cal cottage cheese (110 cals / 462 kJ)

'keep your diet varied and interesting'

be creative

The essence of tasty, nutritious food is variety and freshness. When you go to one of those very posh restaurants where the menu describes every ingredient in each dish, check out the range of products they use — sauces, spices, herbs, seeds are all added to several fresh core ingredients to make the dish truly memorable.

But it isn't just the taste that is so good — variety also improves the nutritional value of the meal; richly coloured vegies are especially nutritious. So instead of sticking a frozen crumbed fish fillet in a frypan and serving it with mashed spuds, try a fresh fish fillet marinated in lemon juice, ginger, garlic, spring onion and a drizzle of sesame oil. Wrap it in foil and stick *that* in the oven. Then steam some whole brussels sprouts with florets of cauliflower and broccoli until they're tender, then dust them with paprika and cracked pepper, and lightly toss them in a non-stick frypan with a spray of extra-virgin olive oil. Both meals are basically fish and vegetables. One is crap and has the nutritional equivalent of soap. The other will make you feel good and let you live a long and slender life. One has three ingredients (if you include the breadcrumbs). The other has twelve ingredients and doesn't taste like old damp newspaper.

The same rule applies to all meals. Breakfast? Half a cup of rolled oats mixed with soy bran, linseed, sliced almonds, sultanas, raisins, chopped dates, sunflower and pumpkin seeds with low-fat milk, half a sliced banana and a dollop of low-cal yoghurt. Getting the picture?

Another reason to be creative with herbs and spices is that when you first start eating wholefood, your tastebuds will tell you it's bland because they're used to loads of salt, sugar and artificial flavours. Don't worry, though. Your tastebuds will come back to life — just as you will when you start eating good food.

be human

Each week I allow myself and my clients to have a treat meal, which includes all their favourite things. One of my friends calls them his 'cheat meals'. Often when we have been out together and a rather delicious-looking dessert turns up, he will say, 'Mish, do ya think it's worth a cheat?' In other words, is this what we *really* want for our treat?

I usually set aside Saturday night for my treat meal. And to counterbalance that, I will train like a woman possessed on Saturday morning. This way I go into Saturday night really looking forward to having a delicious meal with dessert *and* sometimes alcohol, all guilt-free. Then Sunday, I'm back on the healthy-life program. Remember, this is a single treat meal, not a treat day.

12
your
kitchen
makeover

*'your kitchen is ground control
in the war on weight loss!'*

TO SET YOURSELF UP FOR SUCCESS, you'll need to visit the supermarket or produce market at least once a week, and possibly drop into the greengrocer for a top-up. Keep an ongoing shopping list stuck to the fridge door and add to it as you run out of fresh ingredients. When you have a bit more time on the weekend, try visiting local fresh food markets — it's much cheaper and you will always find new and interesting produce to experiment with.

Be smart when storing your vegetables in the fridge: it will make a big difference to how long they last. My mum gave me a great tip: if your breakfast cereal comes in a waxy plastic bag, reuse the bag to store your vegies. Fold down the top and seal with a peg and your vegies will last an entire week, sometimes longer!

Now before I go any further let me get this off my chest: I'm not a vegetarian but I *am* thoughtful about my food choices. I'll buy organic if I can, but it's not a deal-breaker. I won't, however, buy cheap tomatoes that taste like water. Nor will I buy apples that have obviously been on a slow boat from Guadalupe. I absolutely won't buy an egg or meat from a caged bird, and I don't buy endangered fish like red snapper (aka redfish or nannygai), orange roughy (deep sea perch) or swordfish — and that goes for when I'm eating out, too.

Note also that I don't do pre-made fruit juices because they are full of calories. If you like juice, get a juicer and do it yourself, but make sure you add it to your daily calorie tally.

If you are only cooking for one, don't go out and buy *everything* on the shopping lists below — just select what you think you might get through in a week. Also, some foods will be better (and cheaper) in season. It will take you a couple of weeks to find the balance of how much produce to buy so that you have minimal waste. Once you get the hang of it, cooking your favourite quick and easy meals will save you money, make your bum smaller and teach you to appreciate food in a very different way.

fridge

- asparagus (pop into a glass of water and stand in the fridge to last longer)
- carrots
- eggplant
- free-range eggs
- fresh corn
- fruit (okay in the fridge or pantry)
- garlic (fresh or in a jar)
- ginger (fresh or in a jar; I usually freeze my fresh ginger and grate it frozen)
- green vegies (e.g. broccoli, bok choy, choy sum, zucchini)
- low-cal cottage cheese or ricotta cheese
- low-cal yoghurt, no sugar
- low-fat milk (cow or soy) — high-calcium is best
- meat for sandwiches (some people like to have lean deli meat like ham or turkey, though I'm not a big fan, as these tend to be salty. Another option is to cook up an extra chicken breast when you're preparing a main meal, and use that instead)

- multigrain or soy and linseed bread
- onions, leeks
- parmesan (a strong-flavoured cheese like this means you only need use a little)
- salad vegies (e.g. rocket, baby spinach, basil, cucumber, mushroom, celery, capsicum)

freezer

- fish fillets (e.g. white fish, salmon)
- free-range, skinless chicken breasts
- frozen berries (e.g. blueberries or raspberries — they're better value, last longer and are yummy on porridge or yoghurt)
- frozen peas
- lean red meat (e.g. beef fillets, kangaroo fillets, kangaroo sausages)
- multigrain or soy and linseed bread

pantry

- anchovies
- canned beans (e.g. red kidney, chickpeas, butter beans — be sure to rinse them before eating or cooking)
- canned tomatoes
- canned tuna, salmon, sardines
- capers
- chilli sauce (use sparingly)
- couscous
- dried beans (taste better and contain less sugar and salt than canned varieties, but need to be soaked overnight)
- dried pasta
- extra-virgin olive oil (you'll use less because it's strongly flavoured)
- fresh tomatoes (avoid refrigerating fresh tomatoes, they taste better at room temperature)
- herbs and spices (e.g. mixed herbs, paprika, cinnamon, cumin)
- light soy sauce (use sparingly)
- low-cal hot chocolate powder (make sure there are no trans-fats)
- low-GI cereal
- olive oil spray
- olives
- oyster sauce (use sparingly)
- pepper grinder full of black peppercorns
- rice (basmati or brown)
- rolled oats
- seeds (e.g. sesame, pumpkin, sunflower)
- sesame oil
- stock (cartons or cubes — low sodium)
- sultanas
- tomato paste
- tomato-based sauces (no added sugar)
- untoasted muesli
- vinegar for dressings (balsamic, red wine)
- whey protein powder

utensils

I have a deep attachment to a lot of my kitchen bits and pieces because they let me do what I need to do, when I need to do it. My must-haves include:

- a non-stick wok
- two non-stick frying pans — one big, one small
- a good set of stainless-steel saucepans with a steam basket
- a couple of cutting boards
- chef's knife (these have a 6–8 inch blade; if you buy a cheap one you'll be sharpening it forever, so get the best you can afford)
- paring knife
- knife sharpener (not a butcher's steel, get one with rollers)
- silicone utensils (not nylon — it melts and is toxic)
- set of kitchen scales
- measuring cups and spoons
- salad spinner
- airtight containers for leftovers

13
a sample eating plan

'now it's over to you to become a calorie commando!'

WHEN I WORKED AS A PERSONAL TRAINER, and in my work on *The Biggest Loser*, I always put my clients on a nutrition plan that featured a specific calorie quota per day. The calorie quota depended on their gender and weight, and it usually *decreased* gradually as the kilos came off and their lighter bodies needed less fuel for energy.

Most of my big male clients (170+ kilos) started on 1800–1900 calories per day, slowly reducing to 1600 calories as they lost more weight. I usually put my heavy female clients (140+ kilos) on around 1600 calories and got them down to about 1300–1400. If a client had only 5–8 kilos to lose, I put the boys on 1400–1600 calories and the girls on 1200–1300.

Factors such as exercise, hormones and medication can alter these figures (speak to your doctor about this), but for most people, these are the formulas that work.

Personally, I keep my calories between 1200 and 1300 per day, which is light for someone who exercises as much as I do, but with the right food, I never go hungry. In order to stay full and satisfied I eat a lot of low-calorie foods, which is why there's plenty of salad, vegetables, fruit and lean meat in my diet. My portions are not out of control, nor do I go back for seconds. If there are leftovers, I put them in a container for lunch the next day.

I eat throughout the day and I eat very well. The worst thing you can do is skip meals, as it will always come back to haunt you. You always end up feeling starved and it's usually at night — the worst time to take on loads of calories!

I try to stick to my rule of eating like a king for breakfast, a prince for lunch and a pauper for dinner. Of course it doesn't always work, especially on the weekends. But when I know I am going out for dinner I will keep my calories a bit lower during the day so I have some room to move during the evening and don't feel like I'm missing out.

I allow myself only one treat meal and one chocolate treat each week — even so, they really add up, especially if I have alcohol! No wonder people stack on the weight if they eat and drink like this more than once a week! On my treat-meal day I always pump up my training to compensate.

On pages 156–7 you'll find a sample eating plan for a female client wanting to lose 20 kilos in twelve weeks. But anyone can use it — simply adjust the calories to suit your own daily calorie intake goal. You heavy guys out there may need to beef up your breakfasts and lunches (*not* the dinners), increasing the portion sizes to get up to 1800 calories per day. Be sure, though, to gradually decrease your daily intake as the weight starts to come off. I have calculated the calories for each meal, so you can mix and match the meals to get the right quota.

Now it's over to you to become a *calorie commando*! Choose low-calorie wholefood and fill yourself up on it. Memorise the calories of the foods you regularly eat so that you don't have to keep looking them up. **Keep checking in on where you are on your calorie intake as the day progresses.** On *The Biggest Loser*, the first two questions I ask my team members are: 'How many calories have you burnt?' and 'How many calories have you eaten?', and they *always* know. They are making conscious and responsible choices — you can do it, too!

'don't forget — you should be drinking close to 2 litres of water a day, at least 8 big glasses!'

	breakfast	cal	kJ	snack	cal	kJ
day 1	Egg-White Omelette (see p. 164)	70	294	1 medium apple	70	294
	1 chopped pear	70	294			
	1 × 200 g tub low-fat yoghurt	80	336			
	1 reg coffee with low-fat milk	100	420			
	total	320	1344	total	70	294
day 2	½ cup oats, cooked with water	135	567	1 slice fruit toast	100	420
	½ cup low-fat milk	45	189	1 level tbsp low-cal		
	1 small banana, chopped or mashed	65	273	ricotta cheese	30	126
	¼ cup frozen or fresh berries	60	252			
	total	305	1281	total	130	544
day 3	2 slices multigrain toast	180	756	1 medium banana	85	357
	2 tbsp cottage cheese	35	142	1 medium apple	70	294
	1 sliced tomato, pepper, lemon juice	30	126	1 reg coffee with		
	1 kiwifruit	40	168	low-fat milk	100	420
	10 strawberries, sliced	30	126			
	total	315	1323	total	255	1071
day 4	2 boiled eggs	140	588	2 wholegrain crackers	50	210
	2 slices toasted soy & linseed bread	180	756	2 tbsp cottage cheese	60	252
	1 × 200 g tub low-cal yoghurt	80	336	½ sliced pear	45	189
	total	400	1680	total	205	861
day 5	1 kiwifruit	40	168	1 reg coffee with		
	1 nectarine	25	105	low-fat milk	100	420
	1 peach	45	189			
	1 banana	65	273			
	15 grapes	30	126			
	10 strawberries	30	126			
	1 × 200 g tub low-cal yoghurt	80	336			
	total	315	1325	total	100	420
day 6	½ cup untoasted muesli	160	672	1 slice fruit toast	100	420
	1 cup high-calcium low-fat milk	90	378	1 level tbsp low-cal		
	10 chopped strawberries	30	126	ricotta cheese	30	126
				1 reg coffee with		
				low-fat milk	100	420
	total	280	1176	total	230	966
day 7	2 slices toasted soy & linseed bread	180	756	1 large banana	120	504
	2 heaped tbsp cottage cheese	60	252	1 reg coffee with		
	1 cup mushrooms, grilled	20	84	low-fat milk	100	420
	1 onion, grilled	30	126			
	1 tomato, grilled	30	126			
	1 cup English spinach, steamed	5	21			
	total	325	1365	total	220	924

lunch	cal	kJ	snack	cal	kJ	dinner	cal	kJ	total
185 g tin tuna in spring water	200	840	2 wholegrain crackers	50	210	Beef Stir-Fry (see p. 183)	300	1260	
1 medium mixed green salad (rocket, basil, cucumber, capsicum, strawberries, grapes)	60	252	2 tbsp cottage cheese	60	252				1180 cal (4956 kJ)
1 slice soy & linseed bread	90	378	1 large carrot	30	126				
total	350	1470	total	140	588	total	300	1260	
150 g lean chicken breast, grilled	230	996	1 cup fresh strawberries	30	126	150 g salmon steak, grilled	300	1260	
1 medium green leafy salad	60	252				1 cup mixed vegies (broccoli, squash, zucchini, spinach), steamed	50	210	1325 cal (5544 kJ)
1 slice soy & linseed bread	90	378				1 small corn cob	110	462	
total	380	1596	total	30	126	total	460	1932	
2 salmon hand rolls (sushi)	240	1008	2 carrots	40	168	Chicken Drumsticks in Tomato Broth (see p. 194)	330	1386	
1 small Greek salad	120	504	1 large celery stick	2	8				1302 cal (5468 kJ)
total	360	1512	total	42	176	total	330	1386	
Chicken or Beef Stir-Fry (see p. 183)	300	1260	1 peach	45	189	100 g fillet steak, grilled	180	756	
						2 cups mixed vegies (carrots, bok choy, mushrooms, capsicum, eggplant), steamed	120	504	1200 cal (5250 kJ)
total	300	1260	total	45	189	total	300	1260	
Salmon Steak with Rocket and Asparagus (see p. 191)	300	1260	2 wholegrain crackers	50	210	Barbecued Kebabs (see p. 198)	360	1512	
			2 tbsp cottage cheese	60	525				1280 cal (5356 kJ)
			½ sliced pear	45	189				
total	480	2016	total	205	861	total	360	1512	
2 slices soy & linseed bread	180	756	1 peach	45	189	Prawns and Scallops with Orange and Tomato (see p. 190)	260	1092	
1 heaped tbsp cottage cheese	30	126	1 large apple	75	294				
3 slices lean ham	75	315	1 kiwifruit	40	168	1 hot chocolate (made with hot water)	60	252	1310 cal (5502 kJ)
½ tomato	15	63							
½ cup lettuce and grated carrot	20	84							
total	320	1344	total	160	672	total	320	1344	
1 large multigrain roll	160	672	1 × 200 g tub low-fat yoghurt	80	336	Vegetarian Stack (see p. 186)	360	1512	
100 g tuna	90	378							
½ cup salad	20	84							1255 cal (5271 kJ)
total	270	1134	total	80	336	total	360	1512	

14

recipes

'cooking for yourself is an essential skill — and it's easy'

AS I NOTED EARLIER, if you're a foodie and you have plenty of time to spend in the kitchen, these recipes may not be for you. There are some great cookbooks out there that describe how to prepare delicious low-calorie foods, but for me, a lot of the recipes are just too time-consuming. The principle of my cooking is this: I follow simple wholefood recipes, usually with three to five ingredients, and I just add the herbs, spices, seeds, oils, nuts and other bits and pieces as I feel like it (often just what I have left in the fridge or pantry). During the week I simply don't have time to be trussing canard or pureeing twice-cooked white beans. I need my recipes to be quick, delicious and right on my calorie count. On the weekends I might get a bit more adventurous, so I've suggested variations at the end of some of the recipes.

the snowball theory

You know the cartoon where a snowball starts rolling down a mountain and gets bigger and bigger and faster and faster? That's what your metabolism is like once you get it up and running with regular exercise and good nutrition. When you have your one treat meal each week, it's a bit like a single tree standing up in the snow. When the snowball strikes, it takes the tree out, no problem, and just keeps on rolling. The snowball does have a problem, however, if that single tree becomes a forest. Are you hearin' me?

breakfast

These are my top brekkies. Breakfast is a very important part of the day. Too often, I meet people who are trying to lose weight who tell me they skip it entirely – bad move! Having a nutritious meal soon after you get up (or, even better, after your workout first thing) is essential in several ways. Firstly, it gives your metabolism a kick. Your body has not had any fuel while you've been asleep, so if you don't give it something when you wake up it starts to hoard what it has got, meaning your calorie-burning ability is diminished. Having breakfast gets your physiological processes up and running for the day.

Breakfast also gives you energy. Whether it's a workday or a weekend, you're gonna want to be doing things, and so you need energy. Without breakfast, you are going to feel drained by mid-morning, and we know what that means – snacking. If you are energy deficient, you are more likely to reach for a quick-fix, sugar-laden, high-calorie snack to give you a boost. And that's another reason to eat brekkie – it fills you up. If your morning meal is nutritious, balanced and contains a good proportion of wholefoods, you're not going to be distracted by grumbling-tummy syndrome before you get to lunchtime.

So wake up – and eat breakfast!

Use a good-quality wholegrain bread, and choose a ricotta cheese with less than 5 grams of fat per 100 grams. If you don't have fresh herbs, use dried, though halve the quantity.

cottage or ricotta cheese on toast

SERVES 1
PREP 5 mins
CAL PER SERVE 300 (1260 kJ)

2 slices wholegrain
   bread (85 g)
2 teaspoons chopped
   fresh mint or chives
   (or use 1 teaspoon of each)
100 g low-cal ricotta or
   cottage cheese
1 small clove garlic, peeled

1. Toast the bread.

2. Meanwhile, stir the mint or chives through the cheese.

3. Rub the garlic over the toast. Spread the cheese mixture over the toast and serve hot.

This is a big favourite of mine — high in protein, quick to prepare and filling. Wash it down with a nice hot cuppa.

egg-white omelette with toast

SERVES 1
PREP 5 mins
COOK 5 mins
CAL PER SERVE 220 (920 kJ)

5 egg whites
1 spring onion, chopped
freshly ground black pepper
4 cherry tomatoes, halved
olive oil spray
1 slice wholegrain bread
   (45 g), toasted
1 small clove garlic, peeled

1. Whisk the egg whites in a bowl until combined. Add the spring onions, pepper and tomato.

2. Heat a small non-stick frying pan and spray with olive oil. Pour in the egg mixture and cook for 2–3 minutes or until cooked through.

3. Serve on a slice of toasted bread that has been rubbed with garlic.

TIP: If you want, you can add one egg yolk to the omelette mixture for a slightly richer taste. However, be aware that it will add 50–70 calories to your daily count (depending on the size of the egg).

VARIATIONS: Try adding ½ cup baby English spinach or flat-leaf parsley and 3–4 sliced mushrooms to your egg whites. Alternatively, a dash of Tabasco or paprika will give it a kick, or add some fresh thyme or fennel. I love freshly ground fennel seeds – they're so aromatic! Alternatively, steam a handful of baby English spinach, drizzle with lemon juice, sprinkle some sesame seeds on top and serve on the side. You'll deserve it after you've destroyed yourself in the gym or beaten your best time on your Saturday-morning run!

Whenever possible, buy organic free-range eggs. They are a lot more ethical in terms of the treatment of the chickens they come from, are more nutritious than those from caged birds, and simply taste better.

poached egg on toast

SERVES 1
PREP 5 mins
COOK 5 mins
CAL PER SERVE 250 (1050 kJ)

1 tablespoon white vinegar
1 egg
1 tablespoon mashed avocado
1 slice wholegrain bread (45 g), toasted
freshly ground black pepper

1. Half-fill a small saucepan with water and add the vinegar. Bring almost to the boil and just as the little bubbles are rising to the surface, reduce the heat a bit and stir the water vigorously to create a little whirlpool (don't scald yourself!) Carefully crack the egg on the side of the saucepan and release the contents into the middle of the whirlpool – this will stop the white going all over the place. Fish it out with a slotted spoon after 2 minutes for a softie, or 3 minutes for a hardie.

2. Spread the avocado on a piece of toast and pop the egg on top. Bit of ground pepper and there you go! Go easy on the avocado, though – it's loaded with calories.

VARIATIONS: If that all sounds a bit long-winded then simply fry the egg in a pan sprayed with olive oil – the calories are almost the same. Squeeze some lemon juice on the avocado and garnish with chives and watercress, or add grilled tomato and mushrooms or steamed English spinach on the side.

This combination always reminds me of summer.
Take the time to find a good-quality low-cal yoghurt.
Always use fresh fruit, never canned, as canned
is full of sugar.

fruit and yoghurt

1. Spoon the yoghurt into a bowl and place the fruit on top.
   Sprinkle with the chopped mint to serve.

SERVES 1
PREP 5 mins
CAL PER SERVE 300 (1260 kJ)

VARIATION: Add two of the following (these are listed in ascending order of calorie content): strawberries, blueberries, mulberries, fresh figs, cranberries, passionfruit, blackberries, grapes, dates, sunflower seeds, raw almonds, raw cashews and sesame seeds (keep an eye on those nuts and seeds – they have around ten times the calories of grapes!) Add a squeeze of lime juice for extra zing.

1 cup low-cal yoghurt
3 pieces fresh fruit (e.g. banana, kiwifruit, pear), chopped
1 sprig of fresh mint, chopped

Prepare this on the weekend so it's ready for the following week. If making your own muesli is not your idea of fun, grab a bag of untoasted muesli that fits your calorie target (it needs to be no more than 350 calories (1470 kJ) per 100 grams). Beware the ones with buckets of dried fruit as they're super sweet and full of sulphur.

homemade muesli with yoghurt

SERVES 4
PREP 5 mins
CAL PER SERVE 263 (1100 kJ)

2 cups rolled oats
½ cup bran
⅓ cup sunflower seeds
⅓ cup pumpkin seeds (pepitas)
100 g pitted dates, chopped
¼ cup dried currants
1 cup low-fat milk or low-cal
   yoghurt, to serve

1. Combine all the ingredients except milk or yoghurt and store in an airtight container.

2. Place half a cup of muesli in a bowl and add low-fat milk or low-cal yoghurt or both to serve.

TIP: Add a teaspoon of flaxseed into the mix for a morning protein hit.

VARIATION: Serve with strawberries, blueberries or grapes – they're low in calories and delicious.

*This is my all-time favourite winter breakfast.
Make sure the ingredients label reads 'oats' —
nothing else. Rolled or ground, doesn't matter.*

porridge

SERVES 1
PREP 5 mins
COOK 10 mins
CAL PER SERVE 270 (1130 kJ)

½ cup rolled or ground oats
1 cup (250 ml) low-fat milk
1 heaped tablespoon natural
   sultanas (optional)
dollop of honey or brown sugar
   (optional)
sprinkling of ground cinnamon
   (optional)

1. Place the oats and milk in a small saucepan. Bring to the boil, reduce the heat to low and cook for 5 minutes, stirring occasionally.

2. Stir in the sultanas, if using. If it's looking too thick and stodgy, add water. If you like, add a dollop of honey to sweeten, and sprinkle some cinnamon on top.

VARIATIONS: To lower your calorie count, cook the oats in water then add only ¼ cup low-fat milk to serve. To beef it up, mash a banana and cook with the porridge (this will add 100 calories). Serve with a sprig of mint.

mains

These dishes can be prepared as lunches or dinners. Generally, try to keep your lunches pretty generous. As the day progresses, our energy needs change and our metabolism alters in response to the food we eat. So remember, breakfast like a king, lunch like a prince and dine like a pauper.

The quantities I use in many of these recipes are to serve two, but all the dishes are easy enough to adjust up or down as required. Simply scale up if you are feeding the family, or if friends pop by for lunch. And it's always handy to have some leftovers to freeze or refrigerate for another meal.

Don't panic if you don't have everything listed in my recipes. These dishes are pretty adaptable. As long as you have the core ingredients, you can add whatever herbs or vegetables you like – just watch your calories.

Try to go for vegetables that are in season. This is when they are at their finest, chock full of nutrients, and at their cheapest. Eating seasonally also tends to mean vegies are less likely to have come from far and wide to be in the supermarket – making this a more eco-conscious way to eat.

A real 'hands on' dish. You can easily scale this dish up for a larger number of people. I like to just put all the elements in the centre of the table and let everyone construct their own.

Mexican bean tortillas

SERVES 4
PREP 10 mins
COOK 30 mins
CAL PER SERVE 349 (1460 kJ)

1 tablespoon olive oil
1 small onion, finely chopped
½ green capsicum, desseded
   and diced
1 teaspoon ground cumin
1 small red chilli, deseeded
   and finely sliced
400 g can chopped tomatoes
400 g can red kidney beans,
   drained and rinsed
salt and freshly ground
   black pepper
4 wholemeal tortillas
low-cal natural yoghurt,
   to serve
smoked paprika, to serve
½ cup chopped fresh coriander,
   to serve

1. Heat the oil in a large saucepan over medium heat. Add the onion and sauté for 3–4 minutes, until lightly golden. Add the capsicum and cumin and fry for 5 minutes. Add the chilli and tomato, bring to the boil then reduce the heat to low. Simmer for 15 minutes, until the sauce thickens.

2. Add the kidney beans and heat through. Season to taste with salt and pepper.

3. To serve, spoon some of the bean mixture onto each tortilla. Top with a dollop of natural yoghurt and sprinkle with paprika and coriander.

Full of fresh ingredients and so many complementary flavours — perfect for a quick weekend lunch.

chickpea wrap with tahini and yoghurt sauce

SERVES 4
PREP 15 mins
COOK 5 mins
CAL PER SERVE 392 (1640 kJ)

400 g can chickpeas, drained
   and rinsed
2 tomatoes, finely diced
1 Lebanese cucumber, diced
½ red onion, finely diced
2 tablespoons olive oil
salt and freshly ground
   black pepper
4 wholemeal pita breads
2 handfuls rocket
½ cup fresh mint leaves
½ cup fresh flat-leaf parsley

YOGHURT SAUCE
½ cup low-cal natural yoghurt
1 tablespoon tahini
1 small clove garlic, crushed
juice of 1 lemon

1. Combine the chickpeas, tomato, cucumber, onion and oil in a bowl. Season to taste with salt and pepper.

2. To make the tahini and yoghurt sauce, place all the ingredients in a bowl and whisk together.

3. Heat the pita breads in a large frying pan over medium heat until warm.

4. Divide the rocket, mint and parsley between the breads, top with the chickpea mixture then drizzle with the sauce. Roll up tightly to serve.

When tomatoes are in season, they just burst with flavour, and roasting them really brings that out. Combined with crispy fritters and peppery watercress, they make for a luscious lunchtime meal.

potato and corn fritters with roasted tomatoes

SERVES 4
PREP 10 mins
COOK 30 mins
CAL PER SERVE 266 (1110 kJ)

8 cherry tomatoes
500 g floury potatoes
   (e.g. King Edward, Sebago),
   peeled and chopped
2 eggs, separated
¼ cup self-raising flour, sifted
½ cup warm low-fat milk
1 cup corn kernels
pinch of salt
6 fresh mint leaves, chopped
olive oil spray
1 cup watercress (optional)
½ cup low-cal natural yoghurt
   (optional)

1. Preheat the oven to 170°C (150°C fan-forced).

2. Place the tomatoes on a baking tray and roast for 20 minutes.

3. Meanwhile, steam the potatoes over a saucepan of boiling water for 15 minutes, or until tender. Drain well and mash. Stir in the egg yolks, flour, milk, corn, salt and mint. Whisk the egg whites in a separate bowl until stiff peaks form, then gently fold into the potato mixture.

4. Spray a non-stick frying pan with olive oil and place over medium–low heat. Add spoonfuls of the potato mixture and cook for 3–4 minutes each side, turning once, until golden brown. Keep cooked fritters warm in the oven while you make the rest.

5. Serve the fritters with the tomatoes alongside. Top with the watercress and a dollop of natural yoghurt, if using.

TIP: These fritters go well with the String Bean Salad (page 218).

A frittata is a good recipe to have in your repertoire, as it can be adapted for pretty much anything you have at hand. This is one of my favourite flavour combinations.

zucchini and fetta frittata

SERVES 6
PREP 10 mins
COOK 35 mins
CAL PER SERVE 206 (860 kJ)

6 eggs
100 g fetta cheese, crumbled
6 semi-dried tomatoes, chopped
2 tablespoons finely chopped chives
2 tablespoons olive oil
1 red onion, finely diced
2 medium zucchini, diced

1. Preheat the grill to medium–high.

2. Whisk the eggs together in a medium-sized bowl. Stir in the fetta, tomatoes and chives.

3. Heat half the oil in a medium-sized non-stick frying pan over medium heat. Add the onion and sauté for 5 minutes until softened. Add the zucchini and cook for a further 5 minutes, until golden. Pour the egg mixture over the onion and zucchini, shaking the pan a little to spread the ingredients out evenly. Cook for 10–15 minutes, until almost set. Place the pan under the grill for 2–3 minutes, until the top is golden and set.

4. Slide the frittata out of the pan or place a large plate over the pan and carefully turn over to invert the frittata onto the plate.

5. Serve warm or at room temperature, cut into pieces.

TIPS: The frittata will keep in the refrigerator for 2 days. Cover with cling wrap.

I like to serve the frittata with a broccoli and cauliflower side (page 222) when those vegies are in season.

This is a high-calorie meal, so I would never have it for dinner, only for lunch when I've either trained hard in the morning or have a big training session planned for that evening. Don't be tempted to add any more pine nuts. While they are full of good stuff, they are also high in calories.

penne with fetta and lemon

SERVES 2
PREP 10 mins
COOK 15 mins
CAL PER SERVE 480 (2016 kJ)

2 cups penne pasta
1 teaspoon grated lemon zest
2 tablespoons lemon juice
2 tablespoons olive oil
½ cup (60 g) crumbled
   low-cal fetta cheese
1 tablespoon pine nuts, toasted
1 tablespoon chopped fresh
   flat-leaf parsley

1. Cook the pasta in boiling water for 15 minutes or until al dente.

2. Meanwhile combine the lemon zest, juice and olive oil in a jar and shake.

3. Place the cooked penne in a serving bowl, sprinkle the fetta over the top and toss with the pine nuts, parsley and the lemon dressing. Serve immediately.

Stir-fries are a staple in my house. They are quick to prepare, nutritious and the flavour combinations are endless. Typically I include five vegies, three spices and one protein ingredient (meat/tofu). When choosing meat, go for leaner varieties. Personal favourites include kangaroo and chicken breast.

stir-fry

1. Spray a non-stick wok with olive oil and heat until hot. Cook the meat or tofu, stirring constantly for 2 minutes or until browned. The cooking time will vary depending on the type of meat. Remove and set aside in a bowl.

2. Give the wok another light spray, brown the onion and garlic, then toss in the ginger, chilli and vegetables and cook for 2 minutes until tender but still crisp. Overcooked stir-fried vegies taste like crap, so keep them moving in the wok.

3. Add the soy or teriyaki and the meat or tofu, and any juices, and cook for 1 minute.

4. Serve garnished with coriander.

> VARIATIONS: Here are my favourite three key ingredients (protein/vegies/spices) in order of preference:
>
> *Protein:* firm tofu, free-range chicken breast, kangaroo fillet, prawns, baby octopus
>
> *Vegies:* onion, broccoli, baby bok choy, broccolini, red capsicum, snow peas, Chinese mushrooms, spring onions, asparagus, string beans, eggplant, shaved pumpkin, baby corn
>
> *Spices/herbs:* ginger, garlic, chilli, coriander.

SERVES 2
PREP 15 mins
COOK 10 mins
CAL PER SERVE 300 (1260 kJ)

olive oil spray

300 g meat or firm tofu, chopped into 2 cm cubes

1 small onion, peeled and quartered

2 cloves garlic, crushed

1 teaspoon finely grated fresh ginger

1 small red chilli, seeded and finely chopped

300 g mixed vegetables, washed and chopped

1 tablespoon soy or teriyaki sauce

2 tablespoons fresh coriander leaves

183

A satisfyingly hearty meal that goes big on flavour and goodness while dialling down the calorie count. Is there such a thing as a healthy curry? You bet!

vegetable and tofu curry

SERVES 4
PREP 10 mins
COOK 25 mins
CAL PER SERVE 258 (1080 kJ)

2 tablespoons vegetable oil
150 g tofu, sliced
3 cm piece fresh ginger, peeled
    and grated
1 clove garlic, finely chopped
1 teaspoon brown mustard
    seeds
1 tablespoon curry powder
1½ cups (375 ml) low-sodium
    vegetable stock
500 g pumpkin, peeled
    and cubed
1 carrot, diced
200 g cauliflower, cut
    into florets
150 g green beans, trimmed
    and halved
½ cup (125 ml) no-fat
    Greek-style yoghurt,
    plus extra to serve

1. Heat 1 tablespoon of the oil in a medium-sized saucepan over low–medium heat. Fry the tofu for 3 minutes or until golden. Remove from the pan and set aside.

2. Heat the remaining oil in the pan. Add the ginger, garlic, mustard seeds and curry powder. Cook for 1 minute, until aromatic.

3. Add the stock and bring to a simmer. Add the pumpkin and carrot, and cook for 10 minutes. Add the cauliflower and beans and cook for a further 5 minutes. Add the tofu and cook for another 5 minutes, or until all the vegetables are tender and cooked through.

4. Remove from the heat and stir in the yoghurt. Serve with extra yoghurt for dolloping.

As with all of my recipes, don't be constrained by my choice of vegies — chuck in anything you can bake. This is a good recipe to experiment with flavour combinations and with whatever's in season at the time. Because you're going to present it in a stack, you'll need the vegetables to be cut into large pieces.

vegetarian stack

SERVES 2
PREP 15 mins
COOK 40 mins
CAL PER SERVE 360 (1500 kJ)

olive oil spray
1 medium onion, cut into
    4 × 1.5 cm slices
1 × 450 g eggplant, cut
    into 4 × 2 cm rounds
1 × 250 g sweet potato, cut
    into 4 × 2 cm slices
2 large field mushrooms,
    stalk removed
½ red capsicum, deseeded,
    halved
1½ teaspoons chopped
    fresh rosemary
1 teaspoon ground cumin
1 teaspoon smoked paprika
4 cloves garlic, peeled
½ bunch English spinach,
    washed
200 g low-cal ricotta cheese

1. Preheat the oven to 200°C (180°C fan-forced).

2. Heat a non-stick frying pan sprayed with olive oil and brown the onion slices for 2 minutes each side. (To keep them in one piece, use an egg-lifter.) Set aside.

3. Steam the eggplant and sweet potato for 4 minutes or until softened. Place in a lightly oiled baking dish with the onion, mushrooms and capsicum and spray with olive oil. Mix together the rosemary, cumin and paprika and sprinkle over the vegetables. Scatter the garlic cloves around and bake uncovered for 20–25 minutes or until golden. Steam the spinach until just wilted.

4. Place the field mushrooms on two serving plates. Spread the garlic cloves over the mushrooms then layer with the spinach, ricotta, eggplant, onion, capsicum and sweet potato.

TIP: This meal is great with homemade chutney or green tomato relish. I don't usually have time to make my own, but I reckon my nan used to make the best chutneys, so I'll often pick up a jar or two at a market. Be careful, though – they can be very sugary.

Add this little cracker to your 'meals that cook while you're in the shower' collection — it's delicious and low in calories.

baked fish with eggplant

SERVES 2
PREP 10 mins
COOK 45 mins
CAL PER SERVE 300 (1260 kJ)

olive oil, for pan-frying
1 onion, cut into thin wedges
½ (250 g) medium eggplant,
    quartered, thinly sliced
3 tomatoes, chopped
1 teaspoon dried oregano
1 tablespoon drained capers
¼ cup low-cal natural yoghurt
2 × 150 g white fish fillets
small fresh basil leaves,
    to serve

1. Preheat the oven to 180°C (160°C fan-forced).

2. Heat a little olive oil in a non-stick saucepan and cook the onion and eggplant for 5 minutes or until browned. Add the tomato and oregano, then cover and cook over a low heat for 10 minutes.

3. Stir the capers into the yoghurt. Transfer the eggplant mixture to a baking dish, place the fish fillets on top and spoon the yoghurt mixture over the fish. Bake for 20–25 minutes or until the fish flakes easily with a fork.

4. Serve sprinkled with fresh basil.

I love this one! Citrus fruit and fish is such a great combination, and you've got both orange and lime in here. Always go for hand-dived scallops; it's a much more selective and environmentally friendly way of fishing.

prawns and scallops with orange and tomato

SERVES 2
PREP 15 mins
COOK 5 mins
CAL PER SERVE 260 (1100 kJ)

2 cloves garlic, crushed
¼ cup (60 ml) freshly squeezed
   orange juice
1½ tablespoons fresh lime juice
1 tablespoon extra-virgin
   olive oil
1 tablespoon chopped fresh
   basil
1 tablespoon finely chopped
   fresh flat-leaf parsley
freshly ground black pepper
1 large handful (40 g) baby
   rocket leaves
1 orange, peeled, white pith
   removed, segmented
2 oxheart tomatoes
   (or 4 Roma), chopped
olive oil, for pan-frying
6 scallops
6 large green prawns, peeled
   and deveined

1. To make the dressing combine half the garlic, the orange and lime juice, extra-virgin olive oil, basil, parsley and pepper.

2. Arrange the rocket on a platter and scatter the orange and tomato on top.

3. Lightly oil a non-stick frying pan and cook the scallops and prawns for 1–2 minutes each side (prawns will take a little longer) until just cooked through. Arrange over the rocket salad.

4. Add the remaining garlic to the pan and cook for 10 seconds. Pour the garlic and any juices over the salad with the dressing and serve.

Salmon is a great protein provider and is also packed with omega-3 fatty acids, which are essential for brain function. Make sure your fish comes from a sustainable source, preferably wild rather than farmed.

salmon steak with rocket and asparagus

1. Spray a non-stick frying pan with olive oil and heat until hot, pop in the asparagus and cook for 2–3 minutes. Set aside and keep warm.

2. Add the salmon fillets to the pan, skin-side down, and cook for 3 minutes for rare and 4 minutes for well done. Turn them over and cook a further minute.

3. Remove and serve on a bed of baby rocket with the red capsicum and asparagus on the side. Garnish with dill and pepper.

TIP: If asparagus isn't in season, use broccoli. The calorie count is about the same.

VARIATIONS: Add chopped walnuts, thinly sliced fennel bulb and chopped fennel leaves to the rocket salad.

You could substitute ocean trout fillets for the salmon, if you prefer.

SERVES 2
PREP 10 mins
COOK 10 mins
CAL PER SERVE 300 (1260 kJ)

olive oil spray
1 bunch fresh asparagus, trimmed
2 × 150 g fresh salmon fillets
large handful (40 g) baby rocket leaves
½ red capsicum, deseeded and finely sliced
fresh dill fronds, to serve
freshly ground black pepper

This might sound plain, but it's a great dish and makes a light evening meal that fits the 'king, prince, pauper' philosophy beautifully. You can use any firm-fleshed white fish you like; just make sure it's from a sustainable source.

steamed fish and vegetables

SERVES 2
PREP 10 mins
COOK 25 mins
CAL PER SERVE 375 (1575 kJ)

1 tablespoon lemon juice
2 tablespoons olive oil
1 clove garlic, finely chopped
1 spring onion, thinly sliced
   on diagonal
1 teaspoon grated fresh ginger
2 × 150 g white fish fillets
   (e.g. ling, snapper)
1 carrot, julienned
2 corn cobs
100 g broccoli, cut into florets
1 lemon, cut into wedges
   for serving

1. Preheat the oven to 180°C (160°C fan-forced).

2. Make a 'tray' from aluminium foil, leaving enough on one side so that you can cover and seal the contents. Place the tray in a baking dish.

3. Make up a marinade with the lemon juice, olive oil, garlic, spring onion and ginger.

4. Place the fish fillets in the foil tray, pour the marinade over the top, and seal. Bake for 20–25 minutes, depending on the thickness of the fish.

5. Meanwhile, steam the carrot (5 minutes), corn cobs (5 minutes) and broccoli (3 minutes). Serve the fish and vegetables together, drizzling the cooking juices over the top, and with lemon wedges alongside for squeezing.

VARIATION: Serve with other vegetables such as green beans, eggplant or mushrooms (steam for 5 minutes) and bok choy (3 minutes).

I often serve the bok choy separately after marinating it in soy sauce and sprinkling it with sesame seeds (page 223).

This meal is so easy, and any leftovers are good to have cold the following day if you don't have a microwave handy.

chicken drumsticks in tomato broth

SERVES 2
PREP 10 mins
COOK 45 mins
CAL PER SERVE 330 (1386 kJ)

4 chicken drumsticks,
    skin removed
olive oil, for frying
1 onion, thinly sliced
3 cloves garlic, crushed
400 g can chopped tomatoes
150 g button mushrooms,
    quartered
1 sprig fresh thyme
1 teaspoon dried oregano
100 g green beans, trimmed,
    halved

1. Lightly oil a medium saucepan. Add the drumsticks and cook until browned.

2. Add all the remaining ingredients except the beans. Bring to the boil, then reduce the heat and simmer covered for 30 minutes or until the meat is falling off the bones.

3. Add the beans and cook a further 3 minutes or until tender.

TIP: This goes really well with Steamed Kale with Garlic and Lemon (page 219).

VARIATION: For a more substantial meal, serve with brown rice, or with a side dish of steamed vegetables.

Kangaroo meat is fantastic. Not only is it a very environmentally sound choice, it is 98 per cent fat free and very rich in iron (over 46 per cent of your recommended daily allowance in just one serve!) Be sure to let it rest for half as long as you cooked it for, so that when you cut it the juices don't run out leaving you with a dry piece of meat.

chargrilled peppered kangaroo fillets

SERVES 2
PREP 10 mins
COOK 20 mins
CAL PER SERVE 350 (1470 kJ)

2 × 150 g kangaroo fillets
    (if the fillets are thick, slice
    them in half lengthways)
2 teaspoons olive oil
2 sprigs fresh thyme,
    leaves stripped
freshly ground black pepper
1 (300 g) sweet potato,
    thinly sliced
1 bunch bok choy, leaves
    washed, bases trimmed
    and cut in half lengthways
olive oil spray

1. Toss the kangaroo fillets in the olive oil, thyme and black pepper, then cover and leave to marinate in the fridge for a couple of hours, or even overnight.

2. Heat a barbecue or chargrill pan over medium–low heat. Cook the kangaroo fillets for 7–8 minutes each side. Cover and rest for 5 minutes.

3. Meanwhile, cook the sweet potato in a saucepan of boiling water for 2 minutes, or until softened. Remove and drain well. Add the bok choy to the saucepan and cook for 20 seconds. Remove and plunge into a bowl of cold water to stop it losing colour and flavour. Drain well.

4. Lightly spray the sweet potato and bok choy with olive oil and cook on the barbecue over high heat for 2–3 minutes each side or until cooked.

5. Serve the kangaroo, cut into thick slices, on the sweet potato and bok choy.

VARIATION: Marinate 4 fresh figs in ½ cup white wine and a teaspoon of chopped rosemary overnight (at the same time as you marinate the kangaroo). Heat the figs in a pan until soft (about 2 minutes). Drizzle the juice over the meat and serve the figs with the bok choy and sweet potato. This will add around 170 calories to each serve, but should be fine if you're not drinking any alcohol!

The great thing about kebabs is that they're fiddly to eat, which can slow you down and help you feel 'full'. Soak wooden skewers in water for an hour before cooking so they don't burn. Remember, alcohol with barbecued food is strictly a treat. Have plain sparkling mineral water on hand with a sprig of mint for hot summer days.

barbecued kebabs

MAKES 16 skewers
PREP 15 mins
COOK 15 mins
CAL PER SKEWER 120 (500 kJ)

1 red capsicum, deseeded and
   cut into 16 × 3 cm pieces
1 green capsicum, deseeded
   and cut into 16 × 3 cm pieces
8 button mushrooms, halved
1 zucchini, cut into 16 × ½ cm
   rounds
16 cherry tomatoes
300 g chicken breast fillet,
   cut into 16 × 2 cm cubes
1 red onion, cut into 16 wedges
olive oil spray
lemon wedges, for serving

1. Thread a piece of red and green capsicum onto a skewer then ½ a mushroom, a zucchini round, a tomato, a piece of chicken and an onion wedge. Repeat to make 16 skewers.

2. Spray the kebabs with olive oil and cook on a preheated barbecue over medium heat for 12–15 minutes, turning to avoid burning. Serve with lemon wedges alongside for squeezing.

TIP: Serve with a Leafy Green Salad (page 212).

VARIATIONS: Marinate the chicken in olive oil, lemon juice, freshly ground black pepper and chopped thyme for an hour before cooking.

Replace the chicken with prawns or octopus and marinate in olive oil, thyme, chilli and garlic for 1–2 hours.

soups, salads and sides

Soups are the perfect winter warmer, but they are also very adaptable, so you can change them around for what's in season or just what you fancy eating that night. Soups are also great freezer staples. Make extra servings when you are cooking, then freeze in containers for quick reheating – perfect for the end of a hectic weekday. You can heat one on the stovetop or pop it in the microwave. If you are going to have bread with your soup, make sure it's wholemeal, high-protein or multigrain – and even then, don't go mad with it.

Anyone who is serious about weight management needs to be a master of salads. The great thing with salads is that there are no rules, really – keep the ingredients you like handy and add them to suit your mood. Also, see what's in season at the market or supermarket. Fresh beetroot, radishes or asparagus can make delightful additions when they are at their best.

Although usually quite simple, side dishes can really add a complementary combination of tastes and flavours to your primary ingredient, be that a roasted fish, grilled meat, a vegetable bake, or, well, anything! Side dishes are typically a good way to get more vegetables into your meal. As nutritional powerhouses, vegetables should be making up the largest proportion of your diet. A simple side can actually give you large amounts of vitamins, minerals and other elements essential to good health. You can make most side dishes while the main is cooking, meaning you don't have to juggle too many things on the stovetop at once.

Classic comfort food — but this version keeps the calories down. A great option for using up leftover chicken.

chicken noodle soup

SERVES 4
PREP 15 mins
COOK 15 mins
CAL PER SERVE 373 (1560 kJ)

1 L low-sodium chicken stock
2 teaspoons soft brown sugar
2.5 cm piece fresh ginger,
  finely sliced
4 cloves garlic, finely sliced
2 teaspoons fish sauce
200 g rice-stick noodles
½ roast chicken (about 750 g),
  deboned and cut into
  bite-sized pieces
1 cup fresh coriander leaves
1 fresh long red chilli,
  finely sliced (optional)
1 lime, cut into wedges

1. Place the chicken stock, sugar, ginger, garlic and fish sauce in a medium-sized saucepan, and bring to the boil. Reduce the heat to medium and simmer for 10 minutes.

2. Meanwhile, place the noodles in a large bowl and cover with boiling water. Leave for 3–4 minutes, until tender. Drain well.

3. Divide the noodles between serving bowls and arrange the chicken pieces on top of the noodles. Scatter with the coriander leaves, then ladle the stock over. Garnish with chilli (if using) and serve immediately with lime wedges alongside for squeezing.

*Definitely one of the best looking soups around ...
and really good for you as well. Beetroot is a great
provider of antioxidants that help keep your body
functioning correctly. Make extra quantities of
this one and freeze for easy midweek meals.*

borscht

SERVES 6
PREP 15 mins
COOK 1 hour
CAL PER SERVE 118 (495 kJ)

500 g beetroot
1 carrot, peeled and chopped
1 potato, peeled and chopped
1 leek, washed and sliced
1 onion, quartered
¼ cup fresh lemon juice
½ teaspoon allspice
1 tablespoon chopped fresh
   dill, plus extra to serve
2 bay leaves
1.5 L low-sodium vegetable
   stock
salt and freshly ground
   black pepper
low-cal natural yoghurt,
   to serve

1. Wearing rubber gloves to avoid staining your fingers, wash, trim
   and peel the beetroot, then cut into chunks. Place the beetroot,
   carrot, potato, leek, onion, lemon juice, allspice, 1 tablespoon
   of dill and bay leaves in a large saucepan. Pour in the stock.
   Place over medium heat and bring to the boil. Reduce the heat
   to low, cover and simmer for 1 hour, stirring occasionally, or until
   the beetroot is tender.

2. Allow the soup to cool a little, remove the bay leaves, then blend
   in batches in a food processor until smooth. Season with salt and
   pepper to taste. Return to the saucepan and reheat over low heat.

3. Serve with a small dollop of natural yoghurt and a sprinkling of dill.

I love all the different textures in this soup.
A bowl of this on a winter's night — heavenly.

minestrone

SERVES 6
PREP 15 mins
COOK 40 mins
CAL PER SERVE 207 (864 kJ)

olive oil spray
2 cloves garlic, crushed
1 onion, chopped
2 large tomatoes, chopped
2 stalks celery, chopped
2 carrots, peeled and chopped
2 potatoes, peeled and
   chopped
1.25 L low-sodium vegetable
   stock
2 tablespoons tomato paste
1 zucchini, cut into thick slices
½ cup sliced green beans
¾ cup small pasta shapes
400 g can cannellini beans,
   drained and rinsed
3 tablespoons roughly chopped
   flat-leaf parsley, plus extra
   to serve
salt and freshly ground
   black pepper

1. Spray a large saucepan with olive oil and place over medium heat. Add the garlic and onion and sauté for 4–5 minutes, or until soft. Add the tomatoes, celery, carrots, potatoes and stock. Bring to the boil then reduce the heat to low, cover, and simmer for 15 minutes.

2. Stir in the tomato paste, zucchini, green beans, pasta shapes and simmer for a further 15 minutes. Add the cannellini beans and parsley and cook for 5 minutes, or until the beans are heated through. Season with salt and pepper to taste.

3. Serve sprinkled with the extra parsley.

This is a winter favourite, and it freezes well, so make plenty of it for future meals. When reheating it you can also add some meat of your choice, or some extra leafy green vegetables. I often use all my leftover vegies, so it is different every time.

vegetable soup

1. Wash the lentils in cold water then drain.

2. Heat the oil in a large saucepan and cook the leek for 4–5 minutes over medium heat until softened. Add the garlic and cook for 20 seconds. Add the lentils, bay leaves, rosemary and stock and bring to the boil. Reduce the heat to low, cover and cook for 1 hour or until lentils are tender. Add the carrots and parsnip and cook, covered, for 15 minutes, or until tender, adding water as necessary. Add the brussels sprouts, zucchini and beans and cook, covered, a further 4 minutes, or until tender. Discard the rosemary sprig and bay leaves.

VARIATION: Serve with some leafy green vegetables like silverbeet or quartered bok choy on top – the heat from the soup will be enough to cook them through after a couple of minutes.

SERVES 4
PREP 10 mins
COOK 1 hour 25 mins
CAL PER SERVE 250 (1050 kJ)

1 cup brown lentils
2 teaspoons olive oil
1 leek, washed, finely chopped
2 cloves garlic, crushed
4 fresh bay leaves
1 sprig fresh rosemary
1 L low-sodium vegetable stock
3 large carrots, peeled and sliced
1 parsnip, peeled, cut into 1.5 cm cubes
6 brussels sprouts, halved
1 medium zucchini, cut into 1.5 cm cubes
handful green beans, trimmed, cut into 3 cm lengths

Silverbeet is simply packed with vitamins while chickpeas are loaded with minerals. This dish delivers oodles of goodness and bags of flavour.

chickpea, silverbeet, lemon and dill soup

SERVES 4–6
PREP 15 mins
COOK 45 mins
CAL PER SERVE 263 (1100 kJ)

2 tablespoons olive oil
1 onion, finely chopped
2 carrots, diced
2 sticks celery, diced
2 cloves garlic, halved
3 bay leaves
400 g can chickpeas, drained
  and rinsed
1.5 L low-sodium chicken stock
1 lemon, quartered
400 g young silverbeet leaves,
  finely sliced
2 cups fresh dill fronds,
  coarsely chopped

1. Heat the oil in a saucepan over medium heat. Add the onion and cook for 5 minutes, until softened. Add the carrot and celery, stir to combine and cook for 10 minutes. Add the garlic and bay leaves, and cook for 1 minute.

2. Add the chickpeas, stock and lemon quarters to the vegetables. Increase the heat to high and bring to the boil. Reduce the heat to low–medium and simmer gently for 20 minutes. Remove the lemon pieces and bay leaves. Stir in the silverbeet and cook for 5 minutes, until the leaves are wilted.

3. Stir in the dill and serve immediately.

I love the way that the silkiness of the trout combines with the crunch of the snow peas in this dish. Perfect for eating outside on a summer's day.

ocean trout and snow pea salad

SERVES 2
PREP 5 mins
COOK 25 mins
CAL PER SERVE 376 (1570 kJ)

DRESSING
½ cup low-cal natural yoghurt
2 tablespoons freshly
    squeezed lime juice

SALAD
8 baby potatoes
100 g snow peas
250 g skinless ocean trout
1½ cups baby spinach leaves
salt and freshly ground
    black pepper

1. To make the dressing, combine the yoghurt and lime juice in a small bowl.

2. Steam the potatoes over a saucepan of boiling water for 15 minutes, or until tender. Drain and cut in half. Blanch the snow peas in the boiling water for 1 minute.

3. Heat a small non-stick frying pan over medium–high heat and cook the trout for 6–8 minutes, turning after about 5 minutes, or until cooked to your liking. Remove and set aside to cool.

4. Divide the spinach leaves between two bowls. Break the ocean trout into bite-sized pieces and place on top of the leaves, along with the potatoes and snow peas. Drizzle with the dressing and season with salt and pepper to taste.

TIP: This makes a great lunchbox salad. Keep the dressing separate until serving to avoid the leaves going too soggy.

As a rule of thumb I use four staple ingredients in my green salad, and then add whatever bits and pieces I have around. I often buy bags of mixed greens, which usually contain several types of lettuce as well as baby spinach leaves, and I always use cold-pressed extra-virgin olive oil for salads, as it tastes the best.

leafy green salad

SERVES 2
PREP 10 mins
CAL PER SERVE 220 (840 kJ)

100 g mixed salad leaves
2 small tomatoes, quartered
1 Lebanese cucumber,
   quartered lengthways
   and sliced
6 button mushrooms,
   quartered
50 g low-cal fetta cheese,
   crumbled
1 tablespoon chopped fresh
   mint (or to taste)
freshly ground black pepper
1½ tablespoons extra-virgin
   olive oil, for drizzling

1. Combine all the ingredients in a bowl except the oil. Add this after you've served it – that way you can keep the leftovers in the fridge without them going soft and brown.

VARIATIONS: If you fancy a bit more bite in your salad, add a sliced spring onion or replace the mint with basil. You can also sprinkle a few pumpkin seeds on top, or for a sweeter taste, a few grapes or even strawberries. Experiment to find the flavours you like.

One of my all-time faves! It's super quick, low in calories and looks impressive, too. These stacks are great to serve as canapés at a gathering of family or friends.

tomato, bocconcini and basil stacks

1. Arrange the tomato rounds in a single layer on a plate and top each one with a slice of bocconcini and a basil leaf. Combine the olive oil, vinegar and pepper and drizzle over the stacks.

SERVES 2
PREP 10 mins
CAL PER SERVE 300 (1260 kJ)

2 large ripe Roma tomatoes,
   cut into 1 cm thick rounds
150 g bocconcini, sliced into
   1 cm thick rounds
12 whole fresh basil leaves
1 tablespoon extra-virgin
   olive oil
2 teaspoons balsamic vinegar
freshly ground black pepper

This is a favourite of mine, though you'll have to be careful when handling the beetroot not to stain your fingers — try wearing disposable rubber gloves.

beetroot, fetta and walnut salad

SERVES 2
PREP 10 mins
COOK 30 mins
CAL PER SERVE 300 (1260 kJ)

350 g trimmed baby beetroot
1½ tablespoons extra-virgin olive oil
3 teaspoons red-wine vinegar
freshly ground black pepper
1 large handful (40 g) baby rocket
100 g fetta cheese, cubed
30 g walnut halves

1. Steam the baby beetroot for about 30 minutes or until soft, then peel, quarter and allow to cool in a bowl.

2. Mix together the oil, vinegar and pepper and toss with the beetroot.

3. Place the baby rocket in another bowl with the fetta and walnuts.

4. To avoid staining everything red, serve side by side rather than tossing together.

TIPS: When you really need to reduce calories, substitute the olive oil (1½ tablespoons is a whopping 180 calories) with lemon juice.

Leave out the walnuts and the calorie count drops to 200 (840 kJ).

Yum! This is a goodie that I often prepare when I've got the oven on and have an assortment of vegies that need to be used up.

stuffed red capsicums

SERVES 2
PREP 10 mins
COOK 50 mins
CAL PER SERVE 200 (840 kJ)

2 red capsicums
olive oil spray
1 small onion, chopped
1 tomato, chopped
1 (130 g) field mushroom, chopped
1 clove garlic, finely chopped
1 teaspoon chopped fresh oregano (optional)
1 tablespoon pumpkin seeds (optional)
1 tablespoon sunflower seeds (optional)
1 tablespoon chopped fresh flat-leaf parsley (optional)
½ can crushed tomatoes (220 g)
1 clove garlic, extra, crushed
¼ teaspoon dried oregano
freshly ground black pepper

1. Preheat the oven to 180°C (160°C fan-forced).

2. Cut the tops off the capsicums and set aside. Remove the seeds and membrane and trim the base so they will stand upright. Blanch them in a saucepan of boiling water for 3 minutes to soften, and drain well.

3. Spray a non-stick saucepan with olive oil, add the onion and cook over medium heat for 2–3 minutes or until softened. Add the tomato, mushroom and garlic and cook, stirring, for 4 minutes. Feel free to add fresh oregano, pumpkin seeds, sunflower seeds and/or parsley at this point.

4. Stuff the mixture into the blanched capsicums, pop the little lids back on, and stand in an ovenproof dish with a little water in the bottom. Cover and bake for 40 minutes.

5. Meanwhile, place the crushed tomatoes, extra garlic, dried oregano and pepper in the saucepan and stir to combine and heat through. Serve over the stuffed capsicums.

*I love fruit in salads and this is a classic combination.
This dish is so easy and really reminds me of summer.*

rocket and pear salad

1. Place the rocket in a salad bowl and top with the pear slices, cheese and nuts.

2. Mix together the olive oil and lemon juice and pour over the salad.

> TIP: Leaving out the nuts means it comes in at 230 calories (1000 kJ).
>
> VARIATION: Try it with apple instead of pear, particularly if using blue cheese.

SERVES 2
PREP 5 mins
CAL PER SERVE 375 (1575 kJ)

2 handfuls (60 g) baby rocket leaves
1 ripe pear, cored and sliced
40 g shaved parmesan or crumbled blue cheese
50 g pecan nuts or walnuts
1 tablespoon extra-virgin olive oil
2 teaspoons lemon juice

This is all about the crunch — crisp onion, fresh beans and little flavour nuggets of pine nuts. It goes really well with meat dishes.

string bean salad

SERVES 2
PREP 10 mins
COOK 5 mins
CAL PER SERVE 200 (840 kJ)

300 g green beans, trimmed
30 g pine nuts
¼ red onion, finely sliced
½ teaspoon finely grated
    lemon zest
100 g cherry tomatoes, halved
1 tablespoon extra-virgin
    olive oil
1 teaspoon lemon juice
1 teaspoon balsamic vinegar

1. Blanch the beans in a saucepan of boiling water for 1–2 minutes or until just tender. Drain, then refresh in cold water.

2. Toast the pine nuts in a dry frying pan for a few minutes (keep an eye on them as they burn easily). Remove from the heat and combine in a bowl with the beans, onion, lemon zest and cherry tomatoes.

3. Mix together the olive oil, lemon juice and vinegar and drizzle over the salad.

Kale is packed full of vitamins and nutrients and so easy to prepare. I always try to have some on hand when it's in season.

steamed kale with garlic and lemon

1. Steam the kale over a saucepan of boiling water for 5–7 minutes or until tender.

2. Meanwhile, combine the lemon zest and juice, olive oil and garlic in a large bowl. Toss the kale through the dressing and serve immediately.

SERVES 2
PREP 10 mins
COOK 5 mins
CAL PER SERVE 53 (291 kJ)

4 cups (150 g) deveined and
   coarsely chopped kale
2 teaspoons finely grated
   lemon zest
1 tablespoon lemon juice
2 teaspoons olive oil
1 small clove garlic, crushed

Why do we always associate barbecues with meat? They are great for cooking vegetables! The charring that occurs caramelises the natural sugars in the vegies, adding another layer of flavour. Any leftovers will last in the fridge for a day or two.

barbecued vegetables

SERVES 2
PREP 10 mins
COOK 15 mins
CAL PER SERVE 300 (1260 kJ)

1 onion, peeled leaving end
    attached, cut into wedges
1 large slender eggplant,
    thinly sliced lengthways
1 red capsicum, deseeded and
    cut into thick strips
1 zucchini, sliced lengthways
1 field mushroom, thickly
    sliced
2 tablespoons olive oil
2 teaspoons chopped fresh
    rosemary
1 tomato, thickly sliced

1. Place the onion, eggplant, capsicum, zucchini, mushroom and oil in a bowl and toss to coat.

2. Heat a barbecue or chargrill pan over high heat and cook the vegetables for 4–5 minutes each side or until tender. (Put the capsicum on first as it takes the longest to cook.) Add the tomato slices and cook for 1–2 minutes each side.

3. Remove the vegetables, except the tomato, and toss the rosemary through to combine. Serve topped with the tomato.

TIP: You could also serve these vegies as a main, with a dressing of low-fat natural yoghurt mixed with fresh herbs, and some wholemeal flatbreads.

This is a nice way to spice up some steamed vegies! You can try different spices. I sometimes use sumac for a more tangy flavour.

broccoli and cauliflower with paprika

SERVES 2
PREP 5 mins
COOK 15 mins
CAL PER SERVE 120 (500 kJ)

150 g cauliflower, cut into
   bite-sized pieces
150 g broccoli, cut into
   bite-sized pieces
paprika, for dusting
½ lemon, cut into wedges

1. Steam the cauliflower for 8–10 minutes, or until tender. Steam the broccoli for 3–4 minutes, or until tender.

2. Dust the vegetables with paprika.

3. Serve with lemon wedges alongside for squeezing.

Bok choy turns up a lot in my recipes. I love its distinctive flavour, and it also happens to be very nutritious as it is packed with vitamins A and C.

bok choy in light soy with sesame seeds

1. Steam the bok choy for 2–3 minutes or until tender. Transfer to a plate or serving dish.

2. Mix together the soy sauce and sesame oil and pour over the bok choy. Sprinkle with sesame seeds and serve.

SERVES 1
PREP 10 mins
COOK 5 mins
CAL PER SERVE 120 (500 kJ)

1 bunch baby bok choy, washed and quartered, bottoms trimmed but intact
1 tablespoon light soy sauce
½ teaspoon sesame oil
1 tablespoon sesame seeds, toasted

15

eating
out

*'it's your meal,
so have it your way'*

MY INTENTION WITH THIS BOOK is to have
us all cooking more for ourselves, saving on
calories and saving on dollars too! But just
because you're managing your weight doesn't
mean you have to become a social outcast, or
that you should take your calorie counter with
you whenever you're eating out with friends.

I *love* to go out for a meal. And not just
dinner either. There's nothing better than a
Saturday brekkie or a Sunday lunch. The good
news is that with a little knowledge and some
smart food choices, eating out can be thoroughly enjoyable *and* you can keep dropping
the kilos.

The important thing to remember is that
all chefs want their food to taste fabulous so

people will keep coming back, and 'fabulous' often means adding oil, fat, butter or cream. If you eat out *a lot* you will struggle to lose weight. So, choose carefully and be prepared to ask your waiter a few questions.

Here are a few rules when eating out:

- Try to avoid eating out with more than six people. Unless it's a pre-ordered banquet, the food will usually come late, by which time you'll be diving for the bread basket.
- Don't go out to dinner already in starvation mode. It's like watching a train crash. If you're that hungry, grab an apple or a protein shake before you go.
- Ask the waiter not to bring bread to the table, or keep it up the other end.
- Avoid alcohol. Offer to be the driver and go for sparkling mineral water. It's cheaper than alcohol, anyway.
- Don't proclaim to the group that you're on a diet – you're not! You are just choosing to eat better now. And don't get bullied into having something you don't want – it's your body after all.
- Try ordering two entrées instead of an entrée and a main.
- Choose barbecued, grilled or steamed over fried or oven-roasted.
- Ask for any sauces or dressings to be 'on the side' so that you can control how much you eat. If you have no control, then ask for no sauce or dressing.

- Eat slowly. Remember, you don't have to lick the plate clean! If you are satisfied, put your serviette on the plate (even if there is still food on it) as a signal that you're finished and ask the waiter to remove your plate.
- Instead of dessert ask for a low-cal-milk hot chocolate. Sharing a dessert isn't always the best idea if you are like Luke Skywalker with a spoon!

breakfast/brunch

Newspapers, coffee and breakfast — heaven! However, one bad-choice breakfast can ruin an otherwise fantastic weekend of healthy eating and great training. Some of my clients love their Sunday breakfast out so much they use it as their 'treat meal'. However, if your treat meal was Saturday night, choose wisely and specify how you want your breakfast cooked. Don't blow it now!

Smart options include: poached eggs; egg-white omelettes; grilled tomato; grilled mushrooms; wilted spinach; fruit salad; low-cal yoghurt; vegie juices (much less sugar than fruit juice); wholegrain toast (no butter); and coffee (black or with low-fat milk).

Not-so-smart ones include: eggs Benedict; eggs Florentine; scrambled eggs made with cream or full-fat milk; fried eggs; bacon; hash browns; sausages; pancakes; banana bread; muffins; full-fat yoghurt; fruit juices (freshly squeezed is better, but know that a large glass of fresh juice will easily be 200 calories); butter; and coffee with full-fat milk.

pub grub

I live in an area that is renowned for its pubs. It's a fun environment to meet friends and we often end up going to the pub instead of a restaurant. While pubs are notorious for bad food choices, many are now really taking stock of their menus, and if you are smart you can still get a good meal. **As always, it's about choice!** And watch out for the alcohol.

Better choices include a chicken burger (ask for no chips, more salad and only eat half of the burger bun); grilled fish of the day (sauce on the side, no chips, more salad); steak and salad (if the steak is bigger than 200 grams, just don't eat it all, and cut off all the fat); lamb shank (no mash or chips, just vegies or salad); steak sandwich (ditch the bread and ask for more salad).

Meals that will take you to the land of the big bum include: beef burger and chips; nachos; deep-fried calamari; bangers and mash; Guinness pie; and of course, chips and wedges.

seafood

Seafood is a great way to keep the calories low, but as always, you need to stay alert. Sauces and dressings can really add up. Seafood restaurants tend to serve fish with chips, so always ask for 'no chips and more salad'. If you find yourself struggling to say 'no chips', think about that swimsuit!

The best choices are grilled or steamed fish (ask for sauce on the side); barbecued calamari, octopus or scallops; cooked prawns, lobster or crayfish (sauce on the side); oysters natural; and fish broth.

Avoid chips, any deep-fried and/or battered fish (especially beer batter) and anything prepared as a mornay. Particularly high-calorie sauces include lemon butter, aioli, pesto and mayonnaise.

thai

Thai food can be a healthy choice and is lower in calories than most cuisines. However, beware the coconut milk that is used extensively in Thai curries. This stuff is so bad that you may as well rub it straight on your butt, 'cos that's where it's going, baby! And you don't really need a whole bunch of rice with that stir-fry, either. It's dinnertime, so you're about to go to bed, not for a run.

Choose fresh vegetarian spring rolls as an entrée. Other good choices are: steamed vegetable or prawn dumplings; beef, chicken or prawn salads; vegetables in oyster sauce; beef, chicken or seafood stir-fry in oyster, ginger or chilli sauce; green mango barbecued octopus salad; and grilled or barbecued fish.

Dishes to avoid include: curries; anything with peanuts or cashews, especially satay; deep-fried prawns or whitebait; deep-fried spring rolls; duck and pork belly; soft-shell crab (it's usually deep-fried); Pad Thai (unless you are sharing and just have a little); and any fried noodle dish (unless you are sharing and just have a little).

japanese

Again, most of this cuisine is great nutritionally and low in calories. Once you get past the obvious winners like sashimi and sushi, there are a few things to look out for like tempura, crispy-skin fried chicken or mayonnaise-based sauces. Even some teriyaki dishes can be a bit oily, and a bowl of udon noodles and chicken can set you back over 400 calories — ouch!

Dishes that are okay include: sashimi; miso soup; yakitori (barbecued chicken skewers); ebikushi (barbecued prawn skewers); aemono (wilted spinach with miso sauce); teriyaki (beef, chicken or prawn); edamame (soy beans, my favourite! Though pop the beans out of the pod otherwise it can be embarrassing); and sushi (only if sharing with others — as this is rice-based I tend to have it more for lunch than dinner).

Foods that will set you back include fried dishes like tempura and gyoza (dumplings); okonomiyaki (potato pancake with a mayo sauce); noodles (try sharing them and just have a little); and too much boiled rice.

italian

I adore Italian food, but it can be very tricky to find dishes that are not going to load you up with calories! Oh, and you are better off going to a traditional restaurant than heading to a Western-style pizza joint.

Dishes I'd recommend include: barbecued octopus salad; mussels in tomato stock (preferably not too much oil); fish of the day with salad and sauce on the side; minestrone soup; and tomato-based pasta or risotto marinara (for lunch rather than dinner).

Dishes that *will* blow out your calories include: garlic, cheese or herb bread (even bruschetta can be calorie-laden — I don't do any of them); pizza (sorry, but if you want to lose weight, pizza is not on your diet sheet!); veal, chicken or eggplant parmigiana; deep-fried calamari or whitebait; cream or parmesan-based dishes (such as carbonara and pasta with pesto).

indian

Forget it! Most Indian dishes contain ghee, which is liquid butter. Need I say more?

drinking out

Alcohol is full of calories and it's easy to lose count *and* your willpower. Have a couple of drinks with your treat meal and be done with it. Even so, you can make some smart choices with your drink selections. I know one guy who lost weight simply by changing the type of beer he was drinking. And he wasn't even *trying* to lose weight!

The best choices are low-alcohol beer and white spirits with soda and fresh lime. Next would be low-carbohydrate beer, wine and champagne. The worst choices are milky, creamy cocktails and creamed beers.

The bottom line is that to lose weight you just can't afford to be pissed!

staying on track

'be the best you can be — every day'

SO YOU'VE REACHED YOUR GOAL WEIGHT. What happens now? First of all you've got to **close the door** on this part of your life and let it go. Let go of the overweight person you used to be, the history of unhappiness, the photos, the 'fat' clothes — everything. That part of your life is finished. That's not who you are now.

But are you the kind of person who is able to set new goals and refocus? Or are you someone who goes off the rails once they've reached their target weight? I know plenty of people who do the latter — who fall in a heap without the imposed structure of their weight-loss plans and fall back on old habits.

Clearly, it is a lot easier to stay motivated when you've set weight-loss goals and you're actually *seeing* the scale readouts drop every week — nothing motivates like success. But how do you ensure that you keep the weight off? Trust me, there will come a time when there's just no motivation in the tank and you will feel the pull of old behavioural patterns (emotional eating, playing the victim, blaming others for not exercising). What then? Are you going to chuck it in, give up and go back to your old ways? NO! That was the old you. The new you knows that exercising and healthy eating is simply something that you do. Just like you brush your hair, or take a shower every day, **you exercise and you eat well every day.** You know that it's no big drama — it's just what you choose to do in order to have a happy and fulfilling life.

So the day you step on the scales and hit your goal weight, you will give yourself a big pat on the back and then pack yourself off to the gym, following it up with a healthy, nutritious meal. *It just doesn't stop. Ever.* Where you are right now and the things that you have learnt about exercise, about nutrition and about yourself are priceless. It's time for you to pay it forward. This is a gift to pass on to your children, family and friends. You are an inspiration to those around you because you have done what everyone seems to think is impossible.

So what are your next goals? Running a marathon? Climbing Mount Kosciusko? Walking the Kokoda Trail? Hiking in Nepal? There are no limits, especially when you look back at how far you have already come. Get out there and start truly living your life and sharing it with your family and friends. Isn't that what life is about, anyway?

'new you' journal

Here are sample versions of the templates I give my clients to record their progress. Copy them into your journal, or download them from my website, michellebridges.com.au.

daily food/exercise diary

food*	calories in
breakfast	
snack (optional)	
lunch	
snack (optional)	
dinner	

*remember to drink 2 litres of water every day — total

exercise	calories out

basal metabolic rate

total

calorie surplus/deficit

physically I felt:

emotionally I felt:

weekly summary

	Mon	Tue	Wed	Thu	Fri	Sat	Sun	total
calorie surplus/ deficit								

last week's weight	this week's weight	difference

12-week progress chart

	weight	calorie surplus/ deficit	measurements				
			chest	waist	hips	thighs	arms
start							
wk 1							
wk 2							
wk 3							
wk 4							
wk 5							
wk 6							
wk 7							
wk 8							
wk 9							
wk 10							
wk 11							
wk 12							

blood pressure		cholesterol	
start	week 12	start	week 12

acknowledgements

The sign on the front door of my office says 'Michelle Bridges Team'. I chose those words because it serves as a reminder of what I was once told by a Kahuna, a spiritual wise man, when I was in Hawaii one year. He told me that we should always remain humble because we only achieve things in life with the support and love of others.

This book is once again a great example of a lot of wonderful people pulling together and in doing so, achieving something special.

My thanks to Carl Fennessy and the Shine team who got me started with my first series of *The Biggest Loser*. So much of this began with your belief in me all those years ago.

To my amazing publishing team at Penguin Australia – designer Adam Laszczuk, editor Daniel Hudspith and publisher Andrea McNamara – you guys rock! (And thank you for nagging me, Andrea!)

To the amazing Henryk Lobaczewski and Alison Boyle, whose photography skills and hair and makeup artistry conspired so wonderfully to make me look younger. To my stylist Lucia Arias-Martinez – thank you for your patience and vision.

To my friends and partners in the now world-renowned Michelle Bridges 12 Week Body Transformation online program, Tim and Amelia Phillips, OMG – your talents, belief and dedication have contributed to the empowerment of hundreds of thousands of people. We're going to change the world!

I'm probably the only celebrity in the world who actually loves her agent, but that's because she's fabulous! My thanks to the tireless Jane Weston and the Chic Celebrity team, and to Ursula Hufnagl and Pete O'Connell for their wisdom and belief. And to my friend Billy Moore, who's been with me on this journey from the start.

selected references

Blumenthal, J. A. et. al., 'Effects of Exercise Training on Older Patients with Major Depression', *Archives of Internal Medicine*, 25 October 1999.

Cornforth, T., *Women's Health* <www.womenshealth. about.com/cs/gallbladder/a/dietinggallston_2.htm> viewed March 2008.

Drago, L. et al., 'Diabetes and Nutrition: Carbohydrates', *Journal of Clinical Endocrinology & Metabolism*, vol. 93, no. 3 0 <press.endocrine.org/doi/ full/10.1210/jcem.93.3.9995> viewed 2 June 2008.

International Foor Information Council, 'Dietary Fats & Fat Replacers', *IFIC Foundation Media Guide on Food Safety and Nutrition*, 2007–2009 < foodinsight.org> viewed 17 July 2008.

Pavlou et al., 'Effects of Dieting and Exercise on Lean Body Mass, Oxygen Uptake and Strength', *Medicine and Science in Sports and Exercise*, vol. 17, no. 4, August 1985.

index

a

aerobic (cardio) training
circuit training 69, 115
 group fitness classes 69–70
 heart-rate training 68
 interval training 68
 plyometrics 69
 types of exercise 67
 for weight loss 67, 68
 and weight training 70
agility training 106–9
alcohol 141, 149
 calories per gram 139
 drinking when out 226, 227
arms and shoulders
 measuring arms 34
 toning exercises 91–2

b

back stretch 110
back toning exercises 85–6
bad habits 22, 24
basal metabolic rate (BMR) 50
benchmark clothes 35
Body Mass Index 46–7
body types 45
boxing 109
breakfast
 eating out 225
 recipes 162–171
 sample eating plan 156–7

c

calf stretch 112
calorie counter 35, 49
calorie deficit 52–4
calorie expenditure
 chart 51–4
 more burned by heavier
 people 52
 noting in journal 40
 plateauing 68
 in training session 51
calorie quota per day 147
calorie surplus 52–4
calorie-dense food 139
carbohydrates
 burned in weight training 70
 calories per gram 139
 foods rich in 139

low-GI 139
 use in body 139
cardio training see aerobic (cardio)
 training
chest measurements 34
chest stretch 113
chest toning exercises 87–90
child's pose 111
chocolate 25, 64
circuit training 69, 114–15
compound exercises 75
core toning exercises 93–7
cravings 10
cycling 51, 105

d

dairy 145
depression and exercise 60
dinner
 eating out 27, 224–7
 sample eating plan 157
 see also recipes

e

eating
 calorie content 148–9
 daily calorie quotas 147
 eating regularly 147
 low-fat trap 148–9
 portion control 26, 144, 146
 snacks 27, 48–9, 149, 156, 157
 treat meal (weekly) 150, 225
eating out 27, 224–7
 alcohol 225, 227
 breakfast/brunch 225
 Indian 227
 Italian 227
 Japanese 227
 pub grub 226
 rules 225
 seafood 226
 Thai 226
eating plan (sample) 154–7
emotional eating 24–5
energy sources 138
equipment checklist 78
excuses 6–8
 all or nothing approach 26
 living off past glories 30–1
 negative self-talk 27–8

no time 37, 56
 Reward Syndrome 49, 66, 147
exercise
 aerobic (cardio training) 67–8
 benefits 60
 high-intensity 56–7
 informal 66–7
 strength (weight training) 51, 57,
 67, 70
exercises
 compound 75
 golden rules 78
 isolation 75–6
 keeping it simple 76–7
 warming up and stretching 77
 working hard 77
 see also fitness training; flexibility
 training; toning (weight training)

f

facing facts 13–16
family support 38–9
fats
 calorie-dense 140
 calories per gram 139
 good or bad 141
 mono-unsaturated 141
 polyunsaturated 141
 use in body 140
 what to avoid 64
 what to eat 64
fear of failure 12
females
 basal metabolic rate 50
 daily calorie quotas 147, 148,
 154–5
 getting big with weight training 59
 gallstone formation 64–6
fish 145
fitball work 81, 88, 94, 99
fitness classes
 calorie expenditure 51
 group classes 69–70
fitness training
 agility training 106–9
 boxing 109
 cycling 51, 105
 interval training 68
 jogging 51, 101–2
 rowing machine 105

running 101–4
skipping 105
flexibility training
benefits 71
not for weight loss 71
stretching exercises 110–113
types of exercise 71
freezer, stocking 152
fridge, stocking 152
fruit 144

g

gallstones and low calorie diet 64–6
Glycaemic Index (GI) 139
goal-setting 33–4
golden rules of exercise 78
group fitness classes 69–70

h

habit-breaking
chocoholics 25
taking your mind off food 27
hamstring stretch 111
health risk indicators
BMI 46–7
waist measurement 47
healthy weight (BMI) 46, 47
heart rate
maximum heart rate 68, 77
and use of energy source 68
heart-rate monitor 51, 67
heart-rate training 68
high-intensity exercise 56–7
hill runs 103
hip measurements 34
hip stretch 111

i

informal exercise 66–7
inner thigh stretch 112
intensity of training 68
interval training 68
isolation exercises 75–6

j

jogging
calorie expenditure 51
on grass 102
not stopping 62
speed of 102
on treadmill 101, 103
as warm-up or final 'blast' 101
juices 151–2
junk food 7, 137–8

k

kitchen makeover 151
freezer stocking 152
fridge stocking 152
pantry stocking 153
removing temptations 142
utensils 153

l

love your body 33
low calorie diet and gallstones 64–6
lower back stretch 111
lower body toning
bottom halves 79
exercises 80–4
rhythm changes 79
low-fat food 138, 148–9
low-intensity exercise (myths) 56–7
lunch, sample eating plan 157
lying to yourself 10

m

main course recipes 174–99
males
basal metabolic rate 50
daily calorie quotas 147
maximum heart rate (MHR) 68
measurements, how to take 34
meat 144
medication and weight loss 63
missing a training session 57
moderation 26
morning training 37
myths about weight loss 55–9

n

neck stretch 113
negative self-talk 27–8
'new you' journal 39–40, 229–30
nutrient-dense food 138
nuts, grains and seeds 145

o

obesity (BMI) 47
omega-3 141, 145
omega-6 141
organic food 151
over-training 57
overweight
BMI for 47
cost of being 20
as an excuse 20
payoffs for 20

p

pantry, stocking 153
past glories 30–1
personal trainers 76, 109
Pilates 59, 71
plyometrics 69
portion control 26, 144, 146
protein
calories per gram 139
foods rich in 140
use in body 140

q

quadriceps stretch 112

r

recipes, breakfast 161
Cottage or ricotta cheese
on toast 162
Egg-white omelette with toast 164
Fruit and yoghurt 167
Homemade muesli with
yoghurt 168
Poached egg on toast 166
Porridge 170
recipes, mains 173
Baked fish with eggplant 188
Barbecued kebabs 198
Chargrilled peppered kangaroo
fillets 196
Chicken drumsticks in tomato
broth 194
Chickpea wrap with tahini and
yoghurt sauce 176
Mexican bean tortillas 174
Penne with fetta and lemon 182
Potato and corn fritters with
roasted tomatoes 178
Prawns and scallops with orange
and tomato 190
Salmon steak with rocket and
asparagus 191
Steamed fish and vegetables 192
Stir-fry 183
Vegetable and tofu curry 184
Vegetarian stack 186
Zucchini and fetta frittata 180
recipes, soups, salads and sides 201
Barbecued vegetables 220
Beetroot, fetta and walnut
salad 214
Bok choy in light soy with
sesame seeds 223

Borscht 204
Broccoli and cauliflower with
    paprika 222
Chicken noodle soup 207
Chickpea, silverbeet, lemon and
    dill soup 208
Leafy green salad 212
Minestrone 210
Ocean trout and snow pea
    salad 217
Rocket and pear salad 217
Steamed kale with garlic and
    lemon 219
String bean salad 218
Stuffed red capsicums 216
Tomato, bocconcini and basil
    stacks 213
Vegetable soup 207
resistance training *see* weight training
Reward Syndrome 49, 66, 147
rowing machine 105
running
    fast low-step 104
    hill runs 103
    setting your route 102
    speed 101, 102
    stair runs 103
    technique 102
    treadmill interval sprints 104

S
salad recipes 212-8
sample eating plan 154-7
saturated fats 141
second helpings 146
self-awareness 13-16
self-loathing 20, 28
Seven-Day Food Diary 40, 146
shoulder stretch 113
side recipes 219-23
skipping 105
skipping meals 155
sleep 63-4
SMART objectives 33, 34, 52
snacks 149
    calories in 48-9
    sample eating plan 156, 157
soup recipes 202-8
spot-reducing fat 59
stair runs 103
starting off
    aerobic training 67-8
    avoiding reward syndrome 66
    BMI calculation 35, 46

calorie counter 35, 40
clearing out the crap food 39
daily workout time set 37
eating well and regularly 64-6
informal exercise 66-7
medical check-up 63
'new you' journal 39-40
photo 35
realistic target 33
Seven-Day Food Diary 40
sleeping well 63-4
starting measurements 34-5
support network 38-9
target weight calendar 35-7
training buddy 67
weighing yourself 34
strength training *see* weight training
stretch classes
    for flexibility training 71
    part of workout 116
    for weight loss 59
stretching exercises
    importance 113
    sequence 110-113
    see also particular areas
support network 38-9
sweating 59
swimming 51

t
taking responsibility 13-16, 30
target weight calendar 35
The Biggest Loser 2, 52, 72, 154
    competitors 18-19, 28, 52, 142
thigh measurement 34
things to do instead of eating 25
toning (weight training)
    arms and shoulders 91-2
    back 85-6
    chest 87-90
    core 93-7
    lower body 79-84
    prone work 98-100
training
    on an empty stomach 57
    missing a session 57
    over-training 57
    setting daily time for 37
    training hard 77
training buddy 67
trans-fats 141
treadmills 101, 102, 105
treat meal 150, 225
triceps stretch 113

U
underweight (BMI) 47
utensils (kitchen) 153

V
vegetables 143-4
vitamin and mineral supplements 64

W
waist measurement
    health risk indicator 47
    when starting out 34
walking
    calorie expenditure 51
    not for weight loss 55-6, 101
warming up 116
water 64
weight gain
    happening over time 75
weight loss
    aerobic activity best 67
    calculating 52
    goal 33-4, 45
    and lowered BMI 47
    and medication 63
    not through walking 55-6
    realistic expectation 35
    too quick 75
    and weight training 70
weight training
    calorie expenditure 51
    carbohydrate energy 70
    daily 57
    language of 70
    myth of women getting big 59
    as part of workout 115
    and weight loss 70
    see also toning (weight training)
wholefoods 138
workout diary 116
work-out program
    circuit days 69, 115
    progress chart 229, 230
    stretches 116
    12-week program 118-31
    warm-ups 116
    weight days 115
workout time 37, 57

y
yoga
    for flexibility 71
    for weight loss 59